LOCAL GOVERNMENT REFORM IN ENGLAND

This book is dedicated to my wife who has to put up with a lot

Local Government Reform in England 1888-1974

JACK BRAND

CROOM HELM LONDON

ARCHON BOOKS, HAMDEN, CONNECTICUT

© 1974 by Jack Brand
This edition first published in 1974
in Great Britain by Croom Helm Ltd.
2-10 St. John's Road, London SW11
and in the United States of America
as an Archon Book, an imprint of
The Shoe String Press, Inc., Hamden,,
Connecticut 06514

Croom Helm ISBN: 0-85664-130-8

Library of Congress Cataloging in Publication Data

Brand, J.
    Local Government Reform in England 1888-1974
    Includes bibliographical references.
1. Local government — England I. Title.
JS3091.B73   352.042   74-12130
ISBN 0-208-01480-2

Printed by
Redwood Burn Ltd, Trowbridge and Esher.

CONTENTS

PREFACE

This book was started at a time when local government reform was much discussed in universities but not in the town and county halls themselves. Completion of the study was put off several times partly because of weak will and partly because the story really did lack an end until the Act was finally passed. This has now happened and there are no more excuses for delay.

I have asked in this study why local government was so difficult to reform in the years between 1942 and 1972. What were the political and social forces that kept the existing structure in being? I believe that answers to this question tell us something about British politics and about the nature of politics itself and in a final chapter I have tried to make this link.

In preparing this study I have relied on the help and goodwill of many people in central and local government, in the local government associations, and in the universities. It would be difficult to list all of them since I must have spoken to several hundred. It would be equally difficult not to acknowledge that their help was essential to the completion of the work. I hope that they will all accept my thanks. In particular, however, I should like to mention the many hours of discussion I have had with Jim Sharpe of Nuffield College, Oxford.

Perhaps the most important debt of thanks is owed to the MacDougal Trust and the Rowntree Social Services Trust both of which generously provided funds for me to collect information for this work. In both cases the officials and members of the Trusts gave not only money but also advice on the organisation of the data and helped with introductions to important people in local government. Their funding of research into public affairs has played an important part in much of the discussion about the remodelling of reform in this country and it is certainly my hope that such support will go on for a very long time.

Strathclyde University, 1974

THE ARTHUR McDOUGALL TRUST

was formed from a bequest made by the last Sir Robert McDougall LL.D., B.Sc., J.P., who was born in 1871 and died in 1938. He was head of the well-known firm of flour millers and was a man of wide general sympathies; he gave land to the nation and was a strong supporter of the National Trust. He was deeply interested in national and world politics. He took part himself in the campaign for Proportional Representation, and only a month before he died, wrote: 'Democracy should have the fairest and most efficient means of expressing public opinion.' By his Will he gave part of his estate to the Proportional Representation Society after the death of his wife, Lady McDougall, and requested that the fund should be known as 'The Arthur McDougall Fund' in memory of his father. The Proportional Representation Society decided in 1948 that the Testator's memory and intentions would be best served by creating a charitable Trust. The Trust in general exists to 'advance and encourage education in connection with the art of science of government or other branches of political or economic science and to encourage the study of methods of government or civic, commercial or social organisations.'

Secretary:
Robert S.W. Pollard
2 Greycoat Place
London, SW1P 1SD

INTRODUCTION

This book is concerned with the attempts to reform the structure of English local government. For eighty years the same institutions ran local services despite the fact that the nature of these services had completely changed. Why was the reorganisation of the institutions themselves so slow?

There have been many changes in local government since the beginning of the century; some services which used to be locally provided, like electricity, gas and hospitals have been taken over by national bodies. Many others have been added on; the nature of central control has changed several times from rigid supervision of virtually every detail to the more open system of expert Ministry advice.[1] These changes did not, however, touch the principles of the structure of local government. In 1888 the basic organisation of the system was completed and, although there were boundary changes and a few promotions to the ranks of county boroughs, the pattern did not alter. Fundamental criticisms were made of this structure. It was often said that the concept of a county was too small; that the idea of separating a large town (the county borough) from the countryside surrounding it was outdated in days of motor cars and telephones. Many people in the academic world said these things and not a few who were actively involved in local government.[2] These misgivings were felt almost as soon as the present system was brought into being. This book studies the reasons why it took so long to make these basic changes and why these changes finally became a serious possibility.

The reform of local government is not an isolated topic in British politics. In the decade since 1960 there has been far-reaching debate about institutions. A great deal has been written and said about the reform of Parliament.[3] The Civil Service and the Judiciary have both been the subjects of thorough reviews.[4] Secondary education and the universities have had many of their basic values questioned.[5] In virtually all of these fields it has been recognised that some alteration was necessary. At the same time there was great reluctance to take any step towards it. In view of these similarities it may be possible to find some common features which will help to explain this resistance to change.

NOTES

1. See J.A.G. Griffith, *Central Departments and Local Authorities,* Allen and Unwin, London, 1966. Griffith also makes the point that the type and degree of central control varies from service to service.
2. One of the most persistent critics has been Professor W.A. Robson. Such of his writings as *The Development of Local Government,* Allen and Unwin, London, 3rd ed., 1954 and *The Government and Misgovernment of London,* Allen and Unwin, London, 1948, have been influential.
3. See, e.g., Bernard Crick, *The Reform of Parliament,* Weidenfeld and Nicolson, London, 1964.
4. See Royal Commission on the Civil Service. Reference p.000.
5. There has been an enormous amount of writing about secondary education. See R. Pedley, *The Comprehensive School,* Penguin, London, 1969.
   For the universities see *The Robbins Report,* Report of the Committee on Higher Education 1961-63, Cmnd. 2154.

1 THE PROBLEMS OF LOCAL GOVERNMENT AND THE NEEDS OF PLANNING

It is one of the major arguments of this book that local government reform became necessary because of the development of certain local government services. Of all these services none was more important than planning. Indeed, it would have been possible to accommodate all the other changes by making small adjustments to the existing structure. With the advent of new types of planning this was no longer possible.

In this chapter I shall begin with a brief discussion of what was wrong with local government in general. This is ground which has been covered in many books and articles,[1] and I shall not do more than indicate the main heads of the argument. The major part of the discussion will be devoted to showing that it was the developments in planning which made the difference.

The System and its Faults

The English system of local government was set up in 1888 and remained unchanged in its major forms until 1974. The only remarkable thing about this statement is the fact that, almost from its inception, there were indications that it was inadequate and ought to be radically altered. In a paper read before the Fabian Society, for example, H.G. Wells argued for regions.[2] Indeed, regionalism was a favourite theme among the Fabians and among many other radicals commenting on British public policy at this time. What was this local government system which seemed to be so inadequate?

England was divided into forty five counties[3] (forty six with the Greater London Council area which really was, and is, a special case). These 'top-tier' authorities varied widely in size from Lancashire with a population of 2,428,040 to Rutland with 29,680. Below them were urban and rural and municipal borough districts. Whatever the precise nature of the district, the county held the responsibility for the exercise of the major local government powers. Housing was the most important task of the district. The municipal boroughs, which were mostly old towns with fairly large populations, had the widest range of 'secondary' powers; the urban districts came next while the rural districts really had very little powers and most of the local services administered to the inhabitants of these areas were run by the county council directly. Below the county districts in the rural areas the parish remained as an administrative unit, but it had limited powers: the aministration of burial grounds, public parks and such like.

11

Thus most of England was covered by a two-tier system of local government; with the inclusion of the parishes it might be described as three-tiered. However, the very largest towns, seventy nine of them in all, called county boroughs, stood completely outside this arrangement. For administrative purposes the county borough was completely independent. The county had no jurisdiction over the area of the county borough for police services, for road services, for education, for lighting or indeed for any of the local authority services. Thus it was common for a county to have taken out of the centre of it the most important urban area within its geographical boundaries. The county borough was a one-tier local authority. Unlike the county it did not share its local powers with any second-tier body. The town council was the final policy decision-maker for anything which fell within the sphere of local government.

For various reasons this arrangement was inadequate for modern conditions. There were demographic and economic changes and changes in the social philosophy behind the formulation of policy.[4] As local government was set up, it was difficult to adjust to meet these new needs.

Perhaps the most striking feature of local government in the twentieth century has been the continual argument between the counties and the county boroughs. The latter on the whole were attracting population as the result of industrialisation and urbanisation which had been going on for about a century.[5] Soon after 1888 the situation in many of these county boroughs was that their populations had overspilled their boundaries and were living in a ring of suburbs which were legally in the county but from which they (or their menfolk) commuted daily into the city in order to earn their living or to find their entertainment. When the towns, always hungry for more land to build houses or factories, applied for the annexation of these new areas, the counties protested because, apart from the symbolic value of losing these pieces of land, these areas represented a valuable rateable asset which they had no wish to give up. When Private Bill legislation was brought into Parliament to effect boundary changes, objections were often successful. Thus between the two types of local authority there was a continuous dogfight which impeded change. This will be illustrated many times over in the course of this study. Unwillingness to allow adjustment meant that the actual extent of the growing and dynamic urban areas bore little relationship to their administrative boundaries. Houses, shopping centres and factories often sprawled and scattered over more than a dozen jurisdictions within one built-up area with all the dislocation of services and administrative confusion that this entailed. Given the constant pressure by the towns to expand and the efforts of the counties to contain them, the relationship of the two types of authority was polite (and sometimes impolite) antagonism. Some authorities achieved good relationships but for most, the old slogan of the Northern Irish Orangemen 'not an inch' could have been taken over complete.

The effect of this antagonism was that local government was not able to perform many services in an efficient way. An example from the world of education will illustrate one of these problems. If a family lived in a suburb in the county side of the border with a county borough, they might well be expected to send their children several miles away to a county school when the nearest school lay only a couple of minutes down the road on the wrong side of the boundary. The change in the quality of road surfacing and street lighting was often apparent as one crossed from one authority to another. Road works, sewer works and indeed many of the major local government building projects which should have been handled as one large effort covering the whole of the built-up area had to stop at what had become an almost wholly arbitrary line to be taken up again by a new authority with a new building organisation which had had to make new plans with different standards.

If the local authorities had only been required to conduct the same services as they had had at the end of the nineteenth century the situation would have been bad enough. In fact more and more duties were laid upon the counties and county boroughs. They had to make more provision for specialised types of education such as the education of the handicapped and further education. A whole new set of duties in social welfare was heaped upon them. Police and other protective agencies had to operate at a new level of sophistication. In all then, a Victorian model organisation (and one which had had problems from its beginnings) was called on to cope with modern tasks. Its performance was inadequate.

The administrative defects devalued the local authorities in the eyes of the national government officials and politicians who had to monitor the performance of the councils. The confusion of boundaries also meant that as political units local government had very little support from its inhabitants. At least this was the conclusion to be drawn from the low polling figures (sometimes below twenty per cent of the electorate) at local elections. Local government seemed to have lost a great deal of its political credibility.

This rehearsal of the problems of local government gives the outline of the situation. In order to see why the matter came to a head in the mid-'sixties it is necessary to go into the background of these changes in a little more detail. Exactly what were the changes in the British population which caused a new type of urban society? What aspects of it caused the development of a new type of planning? How did this new planning, in turn, make reform possible?

The Changes in the English Population

The increasing size of the population, its urbanisation and industrialisation are the key demographic features. Closely tied to these are the developments in technology which made such a difference to the type and quality of all local authority services. Finally there was a change in attitude to government.[6] Collective responsibility and state intervention had been embraced by only a very small section of the population in the nineteenth century. Since the Second World War these have been accepted by the vast majority. They led to the development of the social welfare services. More important than this, they led to an acceptance of planning, both physical and economic.

It is true that the major changes in urbanisation and industrialisation had taken place in the years before 1888. Between 1801 and 1881 there had almost been a three-fold increase in the population of England and Wales, from 8,893,000 to 25,974,000 while in a similar period of eighty years from 1881 to 1951 it had less than doubled from 25,974,000 to 43,745,000.[7] These latter figures represent a great advance but the movement is not nearly as rapid as in the previous period. The same is true of the proportions of the British population living in towns or employed in manufacturing industry. The rate of change in the nineteenth century was such as to change the United Kingdom from an agricultural economy to a manufacturing one. The trend continued in this century but the pattern was already established.

There were also changes more characteristic of the twentieth century. The most important one was the increase in low density suburbs which were built around every city centre.[8]

The decay of the central areas and even of the earlier residential, middle-class areas forced people out to the periphery. It was not only the unpleasant conditions of the city centres which caused the move. There is a well-established tradition in Britain that the countryside is the best place to live. Town dwellers want to simulate rural conditions even if only by patchwork gardens. The prosperity of the end of the nineteenth century gave an opportunity for the lower middle class to copy the habits of their social superiors.

The end of the nineteenth century saw the first Acts aimed at the rehousing of the working classes.[9] By this time, people who were concerned with these things were aware of the effects of bad housing on health, and local authorities were given powers to build houses for this stratum of society. It was after the First World War that the effects of this legislation became marked. In many towns huge low density suburbs of 'council' houses for the working classes started to spread out.[10] The old system of 'back to back' or, in Scotland, of the tenement, was largely condemned on sanitary grounds. Different styles of building with more light and air were needed. As the nineteenth century went on, the middle and upper classes became aware of the conditions of working-class dwellings. The advance of democracy meant that the sympathies of the more fortunate became wider and it was no longer possible to tolerate the differences in living conditions. In the fifteen years before 1908, half a million acres passed from agricultural land to building use.

The war of 1914-18 made an immense difference. The 'Homes for Heroes' programme, although it was by no means successful in attaining its targets, did set a general tone. Speaking of the period 1918-47, Ashworth says:

Almost everywhere the period saw an enormous multiplication of low density residential suburbs which had been the admired symbol of statutory town planning in its original form.[12]

John Burns, a President of the Local Government Board, spoke of 'the straggling suburb round the ever-changing city'. The extent of the struggle caused serious problems in the provision of roads, sewage and public transportation.

The development of this problem was also characteristic of the twentieth century. Urban workers began to live at greater and greater distances from their offices and factories. Ever since railways were built it has been possible to commute very long distances. The development of the automobile gave even greater flexibility. Commuters could live in villages which previously had contained an overwhelmingly agricultural population. The interpenetration of urban and rural population meant that cities became centres of a complicated network of relationships which called for the control of an overriding authority. The gulf between county and county borough was clearly outdated.

A third twentieth-century development is the conurbation. It is true that many large towns had already been created. On the other hand the super towns or conurbations are of more recent origin. Although the numbers within the boundaries of the central towns have fallen in recent years they have become *centres* of larger population masses than ever before. In short, in certain parts of Britain, there were areas where economic conditions made for extensive development of a whole series of towns whose boundaries expanded into the surrounding countryside to meet each other and eventually form one continuous built-up area. Such a phenomenon is virtually unknown before the twentieth century. In some senses the problems are a continuation of the earlier problems of overspill. On the other hand, there are novel features concerned with transportation and planning which raised special difficulties.

Overspill and Local Government Reform

This new dispersal of the urban population has clear implications for local government. The idea of a county borough as an administrative enclave within the area of a surrounding county seemed anomalous. County dwellers used the services of the town and large numbers of them worked there. To the town dwellers the countryside was easily accessible for recreation. Many of the raw materials upon which their life or comfort depended were drawn from the countryside. Thus a jurisdiction which ended at what had been the edge of the built-up area twenty years before was irrelevant. Any healthy urban economy implied a need for more land to take houses and industry. The health of the national economy itself was seen to depend upon this growth.

These developments had their effect on the operation of all local government services. The growth of population in urban centres put a strain on councils on either side of the county boundary. There was a dislocation of services at this boundary when it would have been more efficient for one or other of the authorities to deal with the whole area. Often the new developments would have provided a base, centred on the urban area, for a range of services much larger than the individual authority could provide. With authority pride and the difficulty of joint administration this was an option which was seldom taken up.

There were, therefore, general problems arising from overspill. For most of the services affected, however, the problems were not acute in the sense of requiring structural reform. Although other services had to take geographical conditions into account they were not so much forced to recognise the factor of geography as were the planners. It might be awkward to adjust school intakes so that only pupils on one's own side of the border came into the schools. It might be a chore to make exchange arrangements with the county. It might be irritating for an engineer to stop building a road at the boundary, but it could be done. Doing it might mean that the local authorities lost some autonomy to the Ministry in order that co-ordination could take place. It might be that they would lose parts of services: some types of roads, for example, where a single standard was essential. Police forces might be combined where law and order required the oversight of a large area. For planning, however, the situation was different. In terms of the new understanding of what was implied by planning, those operating the service came to believe that an advantage was not possible under the conditions of unreformed local government. In making this point one is not arguing whether or not the services actually *could* be run under these conditions. That is an academic argument since, in administration, as in politics, what really counts is what people *believe* is possible or desirable. All types of arrangements *could* have been made even for planning in order to run the service under the old order. The problem was that the will to play with the existing system was gone. Nowhere was this connection held so clearly as in planning. Indeed there is virtually no evidence from the journals or commentary of those responsible for the services that they saw a need for reform. In planning the situation was different. It is, then, to planning that I shall turn to explain the pressure for reorganisation.

Planning and Reform

Because of overspill, local government began to feel the need for planning. It was realised that the limited control of land uses within a town was insufficient. It was impossible to determine these uses since the development and deterioration of the area were so heavily dependent opon factors originating from outside the town across the border with the neighbouring county. The existence of middle-class suburbs or satellite towns led to the deterioration of central city areas, a demand for business and commercial premises and a change in use of many parts of the urban area. The focus changed from the city centre to the whole city region. Planners had to take into account the implications of large overspill populations in the surrounding villages and small towns. They had to cope with the merging of town and country. There were financial implications. There were differences in culture between the large city and the surrounding countryside. The civic pride too of those large towns which seemed to be exporting people and industry across their borders was dented. Thus the problem of planning and ultimately of local government reform was not a straightforward one of deciding how a development map was to be drawn. It had a meaning for the amount of revenue which a local authority could depend upon and, perhaps more important, for the values and symbols held by electors and councillors.

The importance of the cultural gap is related to finance. There is an obvious difference in the way the town-dweller and the countryman live. But it was not because of this that difficulties arose over planning problems and eventually over the reform of local government. In the course of the last century, there was a dramatic fall in the percentage of the population in England employed in agriculture. Thus the areas which were opposed to the big towns were not so much the rural areas as the smaller towns, the independent suburbs and the villages. The controversy in British local government has not been between the town and the country, but rather between the big town and the rest. It is the big towns which have the pressing problems: the slums, the need for redevelopment, the social malaise, above all the desperate hunger for land upon which to build houses and factories. To some extent this is a class problem. Small towns do not have a large working-class population with the concomitant threat to the established values.

Whether the inhabitants of the small town are middle or working class, people from 'the big town' are regarded as rough and in some ways dangerous. They are certainly perceived to demand a large amount of public money for education and social services. If they need houses as well, the threat is even more actuely felt. Any authority within 'range' of these urban monsters feels in danger of being swallowed up. Building around the large centre will engulf the smaller centre and destroy its individuality. When overspill from large towns to smaller authorities is suggested, the proposal is often rejected on the grounds that undesirable elements from the big town will destroy the existing community. When finally it is suggested that the needs of planning make it essential that an entirely new local government system is needed to bring together the big town with its surrounding hinterland, many spokesmen of the smaller authorities suggest that this is simply a device for decanting the problems of the big town on to its innocent and financially more viable brethren. Thus for many in the world of local government it was the large urban areas which were seen as the villains of the piece. Many of the problems concerned within the development of regional plans drawn up by joint committees of local authorities stemmed from the fears of the counties and of the smaller authorities.

This fear of the large city fits in with a common myth in British society. In some way the town (especially the large commercial or industrial town) is unnatural, an evil, whereas the countryside (or the small, tightly-knit town) is natural and pure. The pressures of living in the big town cause mental and physical illness whereas outside life is healthier and society is more independent. Life is not a struggle for existence. This is a theme which is common in literature and art.[12] It often comes into politics, especially when there is an appeal to the 'grass roots'. In many official documents there have been references to these values. Nowhere is this more clear than in the Barlow report on the *Distribution of the Industrial Population*[13] where the strategic dangers of the large conurbations were added to the social and economic pitfalls.

There is another side of the picture. Since at least the middle of the

last century towns have been regarded as the centres of progress, of
civilisation, of the modern world as against the quaint but undynamic
charms of the countryside. There was no doubt that the nineteenth-
century towns were insanitary and in many cases the working-class
areas were positively vile. On the other hand there were many who
were proud to be citizens of the thriving, busty, city states. Asa
Briggs wrote:

> The Victorians began to interest themselves in cities in the late
> 1830s and early 1840s when it was impossible to avoid
> investigation of the urgent urban problems. They were horrified
> and fascinated by the large industrial cities which seemed to
> stand for what a writer in 1840 called 'a system of life constructed
> in a wholly new principle'[14]

But, as Briggs points out, the Victorians were not only interested
in the towns as places where 'improvement' could take place. They
were also proud of these great centres of industry and trade and the
huge public buildings which they put up were an expression of that
feeling. Not only were towns the fount of the economy but, for all
their problems, they were also regarded as the home of democracy.
They would lead the rest of the country to liberty. The idea behind the
1888 Act had been that a democratic system of local government should
be extended to the countryside. This legislation stood in the tradition
of the great Reform Acts which had brought the franchise to an ever
larger proportion of the population.

But if county councillors regarded the city as a threat to their land,
the city councillors were conscious that, with the building of suburbs
and the decay of their central areas, population was draining away to
these new estates just across their borders. A drop in population meant
a fall in status. When slum clearance and the consequent rehousing
called for new working-class housing at lower densities than had
existed in the overcrowded old areas, many cities resisted the
overspill. Their reluctance was not simply to do with a right to collect
rates. In it was involved the idea that the city was diminishing in
prestige as well as population. When overspill extended to industry
as well, an even stiffer fight was mounted.

Overspill and Regional Planning

The difference between the old and new types of planning has been
briefly described. The demographic factors which lay behind this have
also been discussed and with them some of the political factors which
intruded upon the execution of planning and the organisation of
local government. It is now time to pick up the main strands in the
development of planning to see how this function radically affected the

organisation of local government. Two themes stand out: overspill and regional economic planning. In the pages which follow these will be examined in detail since they are the crucial features which altered the nature of planning and with it our idea of what local government could and could not do.

Overspill is partly a problem which sprang from the need to rehouse working-class inhabitants of city centres. This need to provide healthy conditions for poor people was recognised long before the beginning of the twentieth century. One group approached the problem in terms of the design of model towns or villages. This was a tradition which went back at least to the eighteenth century when a landowner or industrialist would build cottages for his tenants or workers.[15] There are many examples of these communities. By the end of the nineteenth century, the ideas had developed sufficiently for Ebenezer Howard to write *Garden Cities of Tomorrow*[16] and to be instrumental in the foundation of Letchworth,[17] a town which certainly was in the tradition of the model villages but on a much larger scale and based on much more carefully thought-out principles.

Although the ideas of a 'garden city' and a 'garden suburb' were important in the development of the theory of planning, they were certainly not important in determining the landscape of British towns and conurbations at the beginning of this century. It has already been pointed out that the most marked characteristic was the sprawl of middle- or working-class estates. This is, of course, a feature which persists to this day. It has also been pointed out that people became concerned about the situation and, from a fairly early stage, remedies were suggested.

At no time was overspill and the problem of urban sprawl more seriously considered than during the last war. The national drive for post-war reconstruction formed an obvious background to this. Perhaps the most important of the documents to be issued was the Barlow Report, the Royal Commission on the Distribution of the Industrial Population. The commissioners recognised that the problem was not simply one of the large cities getting larger. There was a drift not just to the towns in general but towards certain parts of the country which offered better job opportunities and living standards. The enormous conurbations in the South East and the West Midlands increased, causing administrative problems and destroying the countryside. The effect of the draining of population into these areas was that other areas lost population. As they lost population they became less and less attractive, both as places to live in and as sites for new industry. The vicious circle of this process threatened to produce a dangerous imbalance in the distribution of population and in the potentialities of each region for development. Barlow argued that industry had to be diverted from these conurbations which were growing at the expense of the rest of the country and any new building should be subject to strict planning permission. fn

The importance of this report was its recognition of the regional nature of the planning problem; indeed the national problem was recognised. It was not possible to see planning as something which could be tackled within an individual town. The forces which shaped what the town was were regional or even national in their scope and under certain circumstances it might be necessary to control them nationally or regionally. Barlow represented the advanced planning thinking of its time. Many of its premises, such as the rather 'Calvinistic' view of the dangers of the large town and the strong emphasis on the preservation of agricultural land, which was gone into in more detail in the Scott Report,[18] have today been given a different place. Nevertheless, Barlow formed the background to the 1947 Town and Country Planning Act which was perhaps the most advanced piece of planning legislation in the world. Development was made subject to planning permission and the Board of Trade was empowered to control the location of industry by the issue of Industrial Development Certificates. By this means it was hoped to steer medium- and large-scale factory building away from the main overcrowded industrial centres and especially away from London to areas of high unemployment. In so doing it was hoped that the prosperity of the decaying areas could be revived. There was, however, some conflict between the IDC policy and the building of new towns around London.

Thus the Barlow report and the legislation which followed it attempted to control overspill by national and local legislation. Immediately after the war, however, the process was not simply a negative, restricting one. It imposed strong statutory controls but at least as important was the requirement that each planning authority designated by the Act should prepare a Development Plan showing how it envisaged it would expand. Those plans, locally drawn up, had the force of statute once the Minister's approval had been given. The Act marked a new stage in the growth of planning ideas.

As far as ideas for a new type of local government were concerned, this point marks the recognition of regional factors. Put together with the positive attitude towards planning this led to a suggestion that larger units of local government were necessary to plan for the direction of regional forces.

In this post-war period, many of the ideas of regional planning were seen much more clearly than was to be the case in the following decade. This is the period of Abercrombie's plans for the London region and for the Clyde Valley as well as others. It was not the vision of these schemes which was deficient but rather a structure of local government which could not put them into effect. It is also worth remembering that the 1947 Act cut the number of planning authorities from 1441 to 145. Not for the first time or the last, a new type of planning called for a new and larger area. In fact planning powers were pushed from the second to the first tier of local government. Any further move to enlarge the scope of planning could mean either a new local government system or the removal of planning from local government altogether.

The motivation of those who sponsored the Acts was concern for the dangers of unplanned overspill and in Abercrombie's plans there were careful calculations of measures of overspill. People were concerned with the growth of towns and it is not surprising that, along with this, should go the setting up of a Local Government Boundary Commission which was to take quite a radical view of the need for a new local government system. The next government, run by the Conservatives, had a much more limited view of planning. Local government reform was also conceived of in much less radical terms, if at all. Both Macmillan and Sandys, when they were Ministers of Housing and Local Government, operated negative planning systems. For Sandys, the Green Belt which encircled all large towns was to be considered inviolable.[19] For both Sandys and Macmillan it was up to the towns to solve their own problems. They were to do this not by poaching upon the territory of their neighbours but by building to higher densities within their own boundaries. Thus the need for new local authorities would not arise since development would be confined to the areas already under urban development.

Another aspect of this approach to the problem is shown in the Ministers' attitude to new towns. The Labour administration between 1945 and 1951 had developed the new towns on the understanding that they were to draw off some of the surplus populations of large centres. In particular they were concerned with London and their concern was shown in the ring of new towns which were built around the capital. These were to be relatively self-contained units where people could live and work and entertain themselves. It is now well known this was not the way in which the system really worked. The important point is that the government was acting regionally, if not nationally, to tackle a planning problem. The sights had to be raised from the days of pre-war planning. The Conservative administration that took office in 1951 did not pursue the new town policy with any vigour. Compare the New Towns Act of 1946 with the Town Development Act of 1952. Macmillan appeared to feel that there was no need for new towns to take overspill from the large cities. What population could not be accommodated in the higher densities of the cities could be decanted under this later legislation by joint arrangement between towns. There was to be no central help other than some finance for the infra-structure. As compared with the ambitious programme of new town development under Lord Reith, this was to be an arrangement between the two towns for their mutual benefit. The whole conception of the tools which were appropriate to deal with planning and indeed of planning itself were severely limited.

It is not difficult to understand this difference in attitude to planning between the two parties. Its political roots lay in the greater importance for the Conservatives of the rural vote. Interestingly enough, it was exactly the same pressure which forced them into the more timid reform proposals of 1971 which were eventually implemented. Briefly, the two great competitors for land after 1945 were housing and agriculture. The first is clearly an urban need which would be keenly understood by the Labour Party. It was also the dynamic factor, the agent of change which was forcing a reappraisal of the local government system. It was a desperate need in 1945. There had been a great deal of war damage in areas where the housing densities had been highest, such as London and Clydeside. There had been virtually no house-building since 1939.

Equally important was the desire for reconstruction and a better Britain after the war and a rise in expectations of local standards. People were no longer willing to live at the densities which had been common in the slum areas. The solution seemed to be for more housing to be built on agricultural land. Agriculture also had its claim, however. Part of the war effort had been directed to making farms as productive as possible. The difficulties and dangers of getting supplies from abroad had emphasised the need for home-grown food. During the war agricultural efficiency was increased and the proportion of land under cultivation had gone up. Agriculture thus had an important and emotional claim to land. It was this claim which was affronted by the new towns policy and by every proposal for a council house estate. It was claimed that good farming land was too important an asset to be thrown away. When the fortunes of election swung towards the Conservatives in 1951 these arguments were given much more weight.

In effect an expanding urban population had to be rehoused on land already at the disposal of the towns. It was noteworthy that when the 100 per cent development charge on land (which had been imposed by Labour) was removed, farmers were not loath to sell land at a large profit to private builders.

It was, in fact, not possible to support the Macmillan-Sandys negative line in planning for long. Towards the end of the fifties, overspill was inevitable. Many of the arguments put up against it were not as impressive as they seemed. It was also, however, recognised that overspill would have to be planned in a way different from that proposed in the forties.

The most important fact to be accepted was that the urban population was too big for it to be possible to stay within the existing boundaries of the towns. Within the Ministry of Housing and Local Government a paper was prepared by A.C. Powell on the growth of London.[20] What he said applied in lesser degree to virtually every other conurbation in the country.

> We are faced with an industrial extension of the London conurbation stretching in an almost continuous Thames-side belt from Reading to Southend, which provides a base for an even greater fan of development extending to the North, North West and North East along every artery leading outwards from the heart of this new industrial Britain.[21]

The Conservative ministers had tried to ignore the phenomenon or forbid it. Labour ministers had tried to control it by building a ring of new towns. Powell argued that this latter approach was as misguided as the former.

> The economic background of the Barlow report is a thing of the past and planning based on it is outdated. The expanding conurbation is the product of geographic and economic forces too powerful for man to reverse. He can only, within limits, direct them into convenient channels.[22]

The direction of change was irreversible. Powell went further than this to argue that it was absolutely necessary for economic health. His article was a contribution of first-class importance which helped to change the whole attitude of decision-makers in this country towards planning. It brought to public attention the nature of the factors at work, and their strength. It made people face the extent to which the development had taken place and it put the development of London and by implication of other towns in the context of the national economy. In it we see the genesis of the South East Study[23] and of all the subsequent regional planning exercises.

For an explanation of what was happening in London and other big towns we must turn to another important publication written about the same time. Cullingworth's *Housing Needs and Planning Policy*[24] makes it clear that previous estimates of housing requirements had been sadly short of the mark. Barlow's great mistake, indeed the mistake which had been made by virtually all demographers, had been to underestimate the rise in the British population. Instead of settling on a plateau or even declining as had been predicted before the war, the population went on rising. This fact, added to the fall in the average family size, meant that more and more dwelling units would be required.

Writing in 1960, Cullingworth estimated that 'ignoring slum clearance needs it may be that over two million new dwellings will be required during the next twenty years. Taking replacements into account the figure may be over four million'.[25] Thus, even if all replacements for existing households were to be found on cleared sites one would still have to find room for another two million. Overspill seemed to be the only answer.

Cullingworth's book came at a time when there had been very little in the way of central government intervention to aid realistic planning. The attitude of the Conservatives was that no real problem existed. The new towns policy had been allowed to run down. Up to 1958 it had provided only 11,000 houses and up to the same date the Town Development Act had produced only 10,000. Thus Cullingworth's work showed that a great deal more central direction and initiative was necessary to deal with a situation which was more serious than had been feared in previous years.

For political reasons, overspill had not been the preferred way of dealing with the problem. The study *Family and Kinship in East London* by Wilmott and Young[26] had been taken in some quarters to show that people were happier living at high densities, even in the slums, rather than in the impersonality and lack of community of the new council estates. Subsequent research illustrated that, close though the community might be, it simply was not possible to accommodate everyone within the existing boundaries of towns. Planners would have to plan for expanded towns and, since it was admitted that towns had to grow, the case for a new look at local government boundaries became stronger.

The major argument against the solution of overspill had been its costs; especially in terms of agricultural land. At about the same time as the publication of Powell's and Cullingworth's work, other studies called in question the economy of *not* overspilling. One of these was Wibberley's *Agriculture and Urban Growth*.[27] In this it was shown that the cost of agricultural land was not, in fact, as high as had previously been thought. Wibberley argued that there had been a great deal of fuss but less of a loss of really first-rate land than had been feared. The second publication relevant to cost was Stone's paper, 'Economics of Housing and Urban Development'.[28] In the form of cost-benefit analysis he showed that:

> In general situations considered, the scope for using high block residential buildings as a means of reducing the costs of providing housing and its accompanying urban amenities is very limited. The only block height which, at current relative costs, appear in general to fulfil this requirement are three and rather more doubtfully four storey blocks.[29]

He further pointed out that small provincial towns had lower real costs as a location for urban development than older urban centres. This arose partly from lower environment costs, partly from lower prices and partly from the advantage of virgin sites over previously developed sites. Since Stone, like Powell, was a civil servant (in Stone's case at the Building Research Station), his work had a fair chance of being taken seriously by the government.

Regional Planning and Economic Planning

The work on housing was not the only work being done in the field of overspill and urban development. It is impossible to think realistically about homes unless there is some consideration of the jobs which will support these homes. It has already been noticed that the 1947 Town and Country Planning Act gave the Board of Trade powers to channel industry into distressed areas and regions in need of help. Thus at the very beginning of the period there was a recognition of the relationship between economic and physical planning. This leads us to the second of the two themes which are to be developed.

Overspill of houses and overspill of industry cannot always be considered apart. The location of industry involved physical planning although it might have been undertaken for an economic motive. Once we have mentioned economic planning it is impossible to ignore the theme of regionalism which runs through it. Ideas of regionalism in economic planning made it easy to consider physical planning and local government reform in the same terms. The acceptability of regionalism in economics made its transfer to physical planning very easy. If the government decided to encourage development in a backward or declining region then there had to be land on which to build the factories and houses. Thus land use planning was immediately brought in. Unless there was co-operation between those who were creating the regional economic plan and the physical planners there was likely to be confusion and stalemate. However, if there was to be a change in the land use of a region as a result of economic planning and if part of this change comprised the expansion of some of the urban settlements as it almost certainly would, then local government boundaries were bound to be broken. The whole question of reorganisation again came to the fore.

All of these factors put together meant that the government was taking action which would alter local government. No fact was more significant than that civil servants became conscious of the regions and of their needs. Broadly the argument is that adverse economic circumstances forced the government to consider the needs of particular parts of the country. From this it was a short step to viewing the economy as a whole in terms of regional problems and the imbalances of economic activity. We have seen that, in the development areas at least, this had direct effect upon land use and physical planning. No less important was the fact that the concept of a region was being used. Policies were applied regionally, local authorities were brought together to consider the common difficulties which they faced. The fact that the regional ideas was there meant that, in a period when local government was generally considered to be unsatisfactory and when a Commission of Enquiry was already working over its boundaries, reformers were bound to feel that a regional solution for local government might be feasible.

The key to government thinking about regionalism in the early 1960s lies in an attempt to alleviate unemployment. The unemployment policy has changed many times. One of the few common elements was to think in terms of regions because the lack of jobs was worse in certain easily recognised areas. In the 1930s the aim was to create jobs in areas of chronic unemployment and to induce industry to go to the depressed areas (euphemistically called 'special areas'). In 1934 and in the 1936-37 Acts (Special Areas Development and Improvement Acts) Commissioners were appointed for these areas and Trading Estate Companies were set up to buy industrial land and to lease it to private firms for development.

From these measures one can identify three characteristics of the regional policy of the 1930s. It was a rescue operation; a net to catch those parts of the country which had fallen and might fall further. Second, it was a piecemeal approach. The Treasury, the Special Areas Reconstruction Association, the Board of Trade and the Trading Estate Companies were all involved, and there appeared to be little in the way of central planning. Finally, the motive force was the carrot rather than the stick. No firms were directed to the wilderness. A few pre-fabricated factories were erected like oases in the wilderness in the hope of attracting passing industrialists.

The policy of the 1940s was different. Barlow, noted the tendency for industry to drift south to the congested areas and the dependence of the depressed areas on one industry. On this basis the Commission made several proposals. Industry should be dispersed and the government should aim for a balanced industrial development throughout the whole country. In particular the economy of each region should be diversified. Apart from these overall aims urban centres should be developed to banish the squalor that was so characteristic. Finally, a continuous survey should be made of the distribution of the industrial population.

The war temporarily halted this approach but in 1944 an important White Paper on employment was published.[30] What was important about it was the acceptance of Keynesian theory concerning the role of government spending and government responsibility for full employment by 'compensating' the economy where private industry was unable to maintain the level of economic activity. It was on the basis of this document that the 1945 and 1950 Distribution of Industry Acts were founded. They replaced the Special Areas Acts.

The 1945 Act gave the Board of Trade special powers in the newly designated 'Development Areas'. These were the old 'Special Areas' except that they also included the large urban regional centres such as Darlington, Newcastle, Glasgow, etc., which before had been left out of the Special Areas which surrounded them. The Board could acquire land (compulsorily if necessary) and clear derelict land. There were powers to erect buildings for firms to rent. Such Ministries as Transport, Power and Housing could make loans, and grants were also available. Non-profit-making 'estate companies' to administer the schemes were established. Five years after this Act, another in 1950 patched up the situation.

This policy was inhibited under the Conservative governments by a series of squeezes. Unemployment got near the level of pre-war years and thus there was not the same incentive for a vigorous regional policy. As McCrone puts it, 'when the country found itself in balance of payments difficulties and suffering from inflationary pressure, some retrenchment in government expenditure was necessary. Development Area policy was among the casualties'.[31]

In 1958 the situation changed somewhat. A Distribution of Industry (Industrial Finance) Act was passed which increased the amount of financial assistance available and made administration a great deal more flexible. The aim of the Act was to encourage industry to go to areas of 'high and persistent unemployment'. The key change was to emphasise 'persistent'. To qualify for aid, the unemployment rate had to be over four per cent for more than a year. The areas were smaller than before and help more concentrated. Financial inducements were more generously distributed, £9,000,000 being lent to 165 companies in the two years following the Act. In addition to the 'physical' facilities and loans there were controls of a strictly negative type. More use was made of the Industrial Development Certificates. Industry was prevented from further building in the Midland and London regions. Ford, Vauxhall, BMC, and Standard emigrated to Merseyside and Scotland. In 1960 the Local Employment Act ended the Development Areas altogether and substituted 'Development Districts' where pockets of really persistent unemployment were tackled. Industrial Development Certificates were used more strictly. The government took powers to build and rent factories and to give more generous loans to firms moving into the

Development Districts, the Board of Trade being the main instrument for the new policy. Three new management corporations, for England, Scotland and Wales were set up to undertake the transactions in land, the building operations and the provision of basic services.

Policy was certainly more purposeful. On the other hand the concentration was a further step away from Barlow. Then the theme was overall planning. Now, there was a retreat to the rescue operations of the thirties. No one specified an aim for the country as a whole. The government did not look at the regional complex of problems but tried to isolate 'problem areas'. They did not consider the economy in terms of the growth potential of areas, but simply in that they had a social problem (unemployment of a certain level). Other countries, France, for example, saw the problem areas as an essential part of a regional economy and eventually of a national one. The doctrines of Professor Paish, which seemed to dominate Treasury thinking, did not allow for this approach.

The Treasury was not alone in thinking about the state of the British economy. There were economists and political scientists who advocated a longer-term approach in terms of regional development and administration. *The Economist* was a prominent spokesman for the group which argued that fire brigade actions to revive declining industrial areas were not practical. What was required was a recognition that many old urban areas were losing populations because their *raison d'etre* was gone. To restore health it was necessary to study the working of the regional economy as a whole and on the basis of this to see where growth could be most fruitfully encouraged. Such a policy might entail the abandoning of the old mill town or mining village, not an artificial propping by enticing industry which could not operate there at maximum efficiency. Instead, growth points should be selected. New towns should be built which were appropriate to modern conditions. For them communications would be necessary and so would the possibility of developing supportive industries.

This general implication also came out of certain studies which dealt more specifically with the economics of industrial location. Various writers working about this time point out that a firm's decision on where to develop was haphazard and apt to be influenced by factors other than the effect of location upon the profitability of the enterprise. Eversley,[32] for example, showed the great importance of amenity and the pleasantness of the surroundings for those deciding upon new development. Luttrell's[33] massive work in industrial location provided detailed evidence for the first time about the conditions under which it was possible to set up new plant away from the traditional areas in the conurbations. For a small subsidiary branch he suggested that it was necessary to locate within thirty miles of the parent factory, but large units employing over two hundred workers could often be placed anywhere especially if the majority of their workers were skilled. There was no need for them to be tied to London or Birmingham. The cost of transport was a less and less important item.

The work of Eversley and Luttrell drew attention to the need for informed decisions on industrial location. They showed clearly that few firms had known how to go about making these decisions. Their writing came at an important time in that the control by government over location was changing. From the end of the war until about 1951 the movement of industry had been determined largely by the availability of factory space which was mainly in old war factories in the development areas (outside the South East and West Midlands) and therefore under government control. It was fairly easy for the Board of Trade to shape the location of new industrial development. About two-thirds of all moves were to these areas. By 1952 the supply of these buildings had dried up and with them went a great deal of the government's ability to control movement even if it wanted to. There were financial inducements for firms to move to development areas but these were not great enough to make any real difference. In any case it was widely felt that the problems of the development areas had been solved. It was the time when Mr. Macmillan told the country, 'You've never had it so good.' There was high general employment and little feeling that government intervention was necessary. The proportion of industrial moves going to the development areas fell to a quarter of the total.

The period from 1959 onwards was marked by a different pattern. Although there was no immediate and acute employment problem, there was a decreasing demand for manpower in old industries such as agriculture, mining, textiles and shipbuilding. The development areas re-emerged as a problem. It became clear that positive government intervention was needed and therefore powers were taken in 1958, 1960 and 1963 so that by 1965 half the movement of industry was going to the development areas. By the sixties, there was a government commitment to planning in the sense that they tried to encourage development in one part of the country at the expense of areas where expansion had been too exuberant. An interest was created in regional policy in the economic sphere and with it a concern about the way in which local organisation could be set up to deal with it. It was not a great step to think about the implications for local government nor to recognise that economic planning of this kind tied in closely with physical planning. This was a sort of physical and economic planning which local government, because of the way in which boundaries were drawn, was not able to handle.

Such a policy naturally had its difficulties. Not the least were political. Agricultural and country interests could not be expected to be charmed and they were powerful in the reigning Conservative Party. Henry Brooke had to fight a major battle on the Cabinet for Dawley and Skelmersdale, the overspill towns for Birmingham and Liverpool. These were conventional small towns. The *new* school of regional planners were demanding the building of major cities and this elicited even stronger reactions. Nevertheless, the 'new' policy had its adherents, even within the Conservative Party.

In February 1962, the Conservative Central Office published *Challenge and Change*.[34] Though more concerned with physical than with economic planning this pamphlet did not ignore the problems discussed above. Regional planning authorities which were to consist of local authority representatives and independent members appointed by the Minister were recommended. A restricted view of the legitimate limit of government interference with industry was expressed, but interference there should be. Planning should be for social objectives. It should recognise the common interests which existed in many parts of Britain, interests which spread wider than any local authority and yet clearly short of the nation as a whole. These congeries of interests were identified as regions. With all the confusions and difficulties, this idea was becoming ever more important. If it was to be important for economic planning it was only a short step to apply the idea to local government.

The 'Problem' of the Regions

One difficulty for regionalists has been defining the nature and boundaries of a region. Accepting the postulate that such a sub-division of the country would be useful, how big should it be? Should there be fifteen or fifty in Britain?

Many national organisations are organised on a regional basis; usually a different one for each organisation. There are eleven 'standard regions' in England and Wales and these are used by many ministries but others operated before 1964 within modified boundaries. The National Coal Board has eight sales regions. British Rail operates on five regions based on the areas of the old private companies. All of these arrangements are strictly administrative ones. They are methods of organising the work of a bureaucracy centred on London. Some exponents of regionalism argued for a democratic system in which regions would be based on a feeling of regional community. Such a notion had not entered official thinking. The difficulty was to establish the fact that any such regional feeling of community existed anywhere.

In one or two areas, there was just such an awareness which spanned existing local authority boundaries. Scotland and Wales, as national units, clearly qualified and within England itself the North East was notable in this respect. In the beginning of 1962 there existed the North East Development Council, the North East Association for the Arts, the Conurbation Roads Committee, the North East Regional Airport Committee and the Regional Planning Committee for Tyneside. Alongside there was a host of other, less official bodies which drew the region together. The personalities of Dan Smith, the leader of the Labour group on Newcastle City Council, and George Chetwynd of the North East Development Council were considerable factors

The occasion for these factors to become most influential came in the winter of 1962-63 when there was a serious increase in unemployment. One of the hardest hit areas was the North East with a rate of 12 per cent. What was crucial was that in the North East the machinery existed to demand help. Its representatives pressed home the point that in any down-turn of the economy it was the older, poorer industrial regions which suffered most. Even in the best of times the 'crisis' areas always got worse. What happened in this hard winter was that conditions became especially intolerable.

On 9 January 1963, an Admiralty House press notice announced, 'the Lord President has accepted an invitation from the Prime Minister to undertake special responsibility for studying the situation on the spot and advising the government on measures necessary to deal with the present problem of the North East and for ensuring that action authorised by the Cabinet is carried out as quickly and effectively as possible.'

Lord Hailsham, occasionally disguised under a cloth cap, went about his business. William Rees Mogg writing in the *Sunday Times*[35] pointed to the tentative nature of the Lord President's assignment; 'his duty *only* to study, his action *only* to advise', but there was little doubt that this was a new departure. It was not possible now to look at isolated cases of persistent unemployment. This peculiar sort of misery was seen to be the problem of an extended area. It could not be solved by creating new jobs for miners whose pit had been closed. One had to look at the needs of larger parts of the country and try to see the interactions that were going on.

It would be incomplete to see this turn of events out of the context of a move towards national planning. The National Economic Development Council had been set up in 1961. Maudling's budget in May 1963 accepted the NEDC's arguments that government money should be spent on roads, ports, electricity and schools to provide a sub-structure for the development of underdeveloped areas. With these went generous concessions to industry setting up or expanding in these

areas. As *The Economist*[36] argued, however, the method of designating
these areas by their unemployment rates (usually around 4.5 per cent)
was inappropriate. Few people inside the government seem to have
come to terms with the argument that, if the reasons for a population
existing at one point disappeared, then it must simply be allowed to
decline. Perhaps the condition of the Conservative government as a
whole was at fault. There certainly seemed to be a lack of leadership
in the government in many fields of policy. Many writers recognised
that the government had to do a great deal more than simply encourage
industry to go into areas, which the Development Council in the
North East and in Scotland had been doing for several years. For this
kind of work it was necessary to have bodies other than Whitehall
which could solve problems on the spot while retaining the wide
perspective of the regional economy.

In June 1963, commenting on the government's policies, the
Federation of British Industries called for 'strong autonomous regional
organisation' to be set up for areas of high unemployment financed
by the Exchequer to ease the way of the potential investor.

Soon two White Papers were published: one for the North East and
one for Central Scotland.[37] They exemplified the older approach to
the depressed areas. Hailsham seems to have argued that they should be
made physically more attractive. There was very little reference to the
overall economic problems of these parts of Britain. In October,
however, Edward Heath was given a new post. He became Secretary
of State for Industry, Trade and Regional Development, a significant
name. Under him a new department was staffed by senior officials
from the Board of Trade and the Ministries of Housing, Transport,
Power, Health, Education and Public Building and Works. Heath's
approach was a fresh one. The base of his formula for regional health
was industry. In this contrast between planning seen as an arrangement
of physical features and on the other hand as a balancing of all
variables to provide better all-round conditions, there lies the whole
contrast between old and new attitudes to planning. What many
critics questioned was the attitude of mind which tried to draw up
plans for the North East or the South East before the plans for
Britain as a whole had been considered. The government seemed to be
several steps behind Barlow.

Regional or Local Government

The themes of regionalism clearly had a relevance to local government
reform. Any thinking about governmental organisation at less than
national level was bound to lead on to thinking about local government.
The arrangements which were contemplated affected local government

even if there were no further developments since they intruded a level between the town hall or shire hall and London. Anyone could see that these regional arrangements concerned at the moment with economic planning would spill over into physical planning and were bound to become involved with other services which were local government functions. Planning was becoming a more and more important local government function. The pressure of the motor car and the shortage of land with the consequent rise in land prices were all making planning a very 'fashionable' local government service. Despite Sir Keith Joseph's belief that regional government should not be considered in the context of local government,[38] the link was becoming increasingly obvious. As early as 19 July, Ian Gilmour MP sent a letter to *The Times* arguing that the Local Government Commission should stop tinkering with boundaries. It was obvious to him that there would be a need for regional devolution in the seventies and since these large changes were not within the remit of the Commission it should stop wasting its time. A leader in *The Times* on 18 November made much the same point in arguing that the Commission's terms of reference were too narrow, a point which had been pressed by *The Economist* from the very beginning. Again on 18 December 1963, the same newspaper carried a first leader which observed:

An era of active government is about to begin. With the Conservative Party's concession to the principle of planning it is clear that the scope of the government's activities is going to increase greatly whoever wins the next General Election. If regional development is to become a reality, if the recommendations of the Buchanan Report are to be carried out, if wage planning is to succeed, the government will have to play a far larger role than at any time since the Tories took over.

The new Minister, Edward Heath, was a significant choice in terms of what has just been said. He was best known at this time for his impressive handling of negotiations to enter Europe. His star was rising in the Conservative Party but he had also made a considerable impression on his civil service advisers and on the European negotiators. Heath certainly appears to have been impressed with what he saw of the French economic organisation and with the French civil service. His officials also seem to have been struck by the sheer competence of their counterparts. It is not fanciful to suggest that Heath's reforming image and the general move towards structural reorganisation in British government comes from this time. Heath must have been aware that the pull towards Europe was going to make the problems of the South East even more acute, and as MP for Bexley and a man of Kent he had personal experience of that part of the world. Thus in Heath were woven together many of the threads of change that had been spun from 1960. The man who had pressed for modernisation of the government machine had also become the Minister responsible for the development of the regions. Add this to the effects of determined propaganda on the part of the North East and it became clear that the time had come for a new stage in the relations between central and local government.

The work which had been started in these last years of the Conservative government was built upon by Labour when it came into office in 1964. There had always been a group of British socialist thinkers who had advocated regionalism of one sort or another. H.G. Wells' paper on Administrative Areas is an early example but in more recent times Professor Robson and Professor Self had written upon the subject.[39] This approach, therefore, came easily to the new government as did the idea of planning in general. The 1966 Industrial Development Act declared over 40 per cent of the surface of Britain to be areas in need of particular attention. It was no longer necessary for an area to have a 4.5 per cent unemployment rate for it to receive aid and other parts of the country where there might be more potential for growth were not excluded. The fact that the areas were wider meant that the government could choose for investment places where there was a real chance of growth. Labour shifted the emphasis in a way which allowed for more realistic economic planning. The idea of regional planning was an essential part of this.

The final contribution of Labour from the field of economic planning bears out this point. It was Labour which, during the election campaign of October 1964, had emphasised its promise of regional planning. They were committed to regionalism. Sir Keith Joseph outlined similar plans but it was Labour which implemented them. Within a short time, the regional arrangements were announced. In each of the eight regions there were to be Regional Economic Boards made up of senior civial servants from various departments working in the region and chaired by a representative of the Department of Economic Affairs with the rank of Under-Secretary. Alongside, there would be the Regional Economic Councils made up of representatives of industry, the trade unions, the professions, local government and the universities. In a statement to Parliament, the First Secretary of State made it clear what jobs would be done by these bodies.

> The purpose of the Regional Councils and Boards . . . is to provide effective machinery for regional economic planning within the framework of the National Plan for Economic Development . . . The Economic Planning Councils will be concerned with broad strategy on regional development and the best use of the region's resources. Their principal function

will be to assist in the formulation of regional plans and to advise on their creation. They will not affect the existing powers and responsibilities of local authorities or existing Ministerial responsibilities.[40]

A structure now existed which, although part of the national government, was a model for a new type of sub-national organisation. Whatever the failings of the economic regionalisation this model was soon to be picked up for local government.

NOTES

1. See, for example, W.A. Robson, *The Development of Local Government,* 3rd rev. ed., Allen and Unwin, London, 1954; or W.A. Robson, *Local Government in Crisis,* Allen and Unwin, London, 1966, or, W. Wiseman (ed.), *Local Government in England, 1958-69,* Routledge, London, 1970.
2. Printed as an appendix to H.G. Wells, *Mankind in the Making,* Chapman and Hall, London, 1963.
3. A good account of the system is to be found in J. Maud and S. Finer, *Local Government in England and Wales,* Oxford University Press, London, 1953.
4. An excellent statement of these changes is still to be found in Robson, ibid., but see also Peter Self, *Cities in Flood,* Faber and Faber, London, 1961.
5. Asa Briggs discusses this in *Victorian Cities,* Odhams, London, 1963.
6. The Keynesian Revolution had taken place and the work of Lord Beveridge changed many ideas about the welfare state.
7. These figures are drawn from the annual reports of the Registrar General.
8. This is well treated in Self.
9. For examples, Housing of the Working Classes Act, 1890.
10. See B. Cullingworth, *Town and Country Planning in Britain,* Allen and Unwin, London, 1972, pp. 20-21.
11. *The Genesis of Modern British Town Planning,* Routledge, London, 1954, p.92.
12. It is, of course, especially true of romantic literature. William Morris in *News from Nowhere* certainly expresses it, but it is present in Dickens and many other authors.
13. Cmnd. 6153, HMSO, London, 1940.
14. Ibid., p.12.
15. New Lanark is probably the best example.
16. *Garden Cities of Tomorrow,* Faber and Faber, London, 1960.
17. Founded in 1903.
18. *Committee on Land Utilisation in Rural Areas,* Cmnd. 6378, HMSO, London, 1941.

19.   Ministry of Housing and Local Government Circular 42/55, HMSO HMSO, London, 1955.
20.   The Recent Development of Greater London, *The Advancement of Science,* Vol. XVII, No. 65, 1960, pp.76-86.
21.   Ibid., p.84.
22.   Ibid., p.85.
23.   Ministry of Housing and Local Government, HMSO, London, 1964.
24.   London, Longmans, 1960.
25.   Ibid., p.59.
26.   Routledge, London, 1969.
27.   G.P. Wibberley, *Agriculture and Urban Growth,* Michael Joseph, London, 1959.
28.   *Journal of the Royal Statistical Society,* vol. 122, p.4, pp.417-76.
29.   Ibid., p.450.
30.   Cmnd. 6609/44, HMSO, London, 1944.
31.   *Regional Policy in Britain,* Allen and Unwin, London, 1970, p.115.
32.   D. Eversley, *Population Growth and Planning Policy,* Cass, London, 1965.
33.   *Factory, Location and Industrial Movement,* N.I.E.S.R, London, 1962.
34.   Conservative Political Centre, No. 247.
35.   13 January 1963.
36.   11 May 1963.
37.   *Central Scotland: a Programme for Development and Growth,* Cmnd. 2188, HMSO, 1963. *The North East,* Cmnd. 2206, HMSO, London, 1963.
38.   See Local Authorities and the Regions, *Public Administration,* Vol. 42, No. 3, 1964, pp.215-26.
39.   Self and Robson, ibid.
40.   House of Commons Debates, vol. 703, col. 1829.

2   THE MINISTRIES AND LOCAL GOVERNMENT REFORM

We start the study of the participants in local government reform from the perspective of the central government. In large measure it was from this source that the initiative came. Consequently we cannot understand the reaction of the others until we understand what they reacted to. Secondly, this topic cannot be understood out of the context of national politics.

Local Government Reorganisation in Wartime

The first moves towards reform came at the beginning of the war. In 1941 a Committee of the British War Cabinet, chaired by Arthur Greenwood, dealing with reconstruction turned to the structure of local government.

At this time many departments were involved in regional administration which coloured official thinking. Many ministries co-operated in the system whereby the country was divided into twelve regions with a Regional Commissioner at the head. This official, sometimes a politician but at any rate a fairly well-known figure, had the task of leading a 'little Whitehall' at the sub-national level. Richard Titmuss explains the origin of the system:

during the pre-war years when Civil Defence and allied questions were being studied, the importance of communication and administration was repeatedly emphasised. The regional system arose from such considerations; another argument for decentralisation was the possibility that the seat of government might have to be moved from London.[1]

Although the system may have had its origin in civil defence and the contingencies of bombing and invasion, it soon covered a host of ordinary local government problems. In theory the offices of the Regional Commissioner were clearing houses for communications. They were supposed to co-ordinate and if necessary knock together the heads of local authorities. In practice their power to do this depended on the personalities in the Regional Office and the local authorities concerned. Nevertheless Whitehall clearly felt that regional organisation was useful. Again Titmuss explains: 'the problems of boundaries came to be very important during the war. It affected many of the emergency social services, the evacuation scheme, the mail service and to a lesser degree the emergency hospital scheme.'[2]

One problem was that local government boundaries were based upon the assumption of static populations. In war, this was not the case. War work or evacuation moved people all the time and it was not possible to demand a set waiting period on a housing list before essential war workers could be housed. Our effort to win the war could not tolerate the niceties with which local authorities held each other, the ministries and the public at arm's length.

The crisis conditions of wartime offered an opportunity to solve a problem which had existed since the abortive reforms of 1888. A number of articles on regionalisation had been published around this time including one by W.A. Robson[3] entitled 'We must regionalise or perish.' This summed up the position taken in 'The Development of Local Government',[4] In May 1941, influenced no doubt by its recent experience of these 'little Whitehalls', the Minstry of Health circulated to the local government associations its 'Notes on Regionalism', These included a discussion of ways in which regional councils could be set up. It outlined a country-wide system of elected bodies running many of the existing local services. These moves indicate that there was a feeling in many departments that the structure of local government should be changed. In November, it was announced that Greenwood had called on Sir William Jowitt, the Solicitor General, to undertake a preliminary survey of certain problems of local government.

The work of the enquiry was started at a propitious time for reform in that there were many new ideas around in British society. Conversely there were other great needs which had to be met as quickly as possible. Houses had to be built to replace those which had been bombed out or found to be deficient. As in the First World War the health of the soldiers cast new light on the deprivations of working-class life. The National Health Service was not exclusively an idea of the Labour Party. The 1944 Education Act was an all-party measure. In almost every field of administration which concerned local government, new plans were being made and to a great extent they were made in consultation with and by the agreement of the local authorities. There was, however, to be no agreement about reform of the *institutions*. There were other points which made reform difficult. The Bills on, for example, education and social welfare could be treated as incremental changes upon the existing state of the services. In education, the 1944 Act made great steps forward but the type of two-tier education which it required had already been initiated by some local authorities. Local government reform, on the other hand, was a step in the dark. Moreover, the development of these services was being demanded by powerful pressure groups; in education, for example, by the National Union of Teachers, and the Association of Education Committees. There was no such powerful group pressing for local government reform. Finally, whereas there were various spending departments within the government whose job it was to look after education, health etc., the appropriate part of the bureaucracy to study and advise on structural questions was not clearly defined. In all, there was political pressure to set up the new services and this had priority over the reorganisation of structure. With each department and all the political parties clamouring for new Acts to improve these services the government *had* to set them up as quickly as possible. It was predictable that a thorough reform of the structure would take second place.

By the middle of 1944 the conclusions of the enquiry into local government began to be known. The Minister of Health, with responsibility for local government was at this time Sir Henry Willink. He had been the wartime Special Commissioner for the co-ordination of housing in the London region and as such had to deal with over a hundred authorities responsible for the rehousing of those who had been bombed out. Other than this he had no experience of local government. His main jobs as Minister were the solution of the housing problem which was, of course, acute and the laying of preliminary plans for the National Health Service. The Ministry was grossly overworked. It was not surprising that radical plans for local government were not pressed from this end. Instead it was proposed to set up a local government boundary commission.

The decision to have the commission originated from the report to the Cabinet Committee. It was envisaged from the very start as a body which would readjust boundaries, but within the existing framework. On 3 August 1944 the Minister made a statement in Parliament.

> The government are satisfied that, within the general framework of the county and county borough system, there is need and scope for improvements and in particular for amending the machinery of the Local Government Act 1933 relating to adjustments of status, boundaries and areas.[5]

He promised to open discussions with the local government associations in September.

Discussions were held in the latter half of the year and the White Paper *Local Government in England and Wales during the Period of Reconstruction*[6] duly appeared in January 1945. In it a Local Government Boundary Commission was proposed. The report of the Association of Municipal Corporations' special committee on reconstruction pointed out that the government did not consult the

local government associations on the distribution of functions.
Apparently this subject was too important to trust to such an angry
sea. It involved national policy and in the long run it was a much more
'party political' question than that of local government reform. In the
debate on the White Paper, Willink expressed the view that 100,000
was the minimum population for a county borough.

Thus at the end of the war the stage seemed to be set for a review
of boundaries which would mean the extension of many urban
authorities but also the demotion of many county boroughs.

The movement for local government reform in Britain fell into two
phases. There is, first, an attempt by the government to look at the
machinery of government in Britain as a whole. Jowitt's appointment
by the Cabinet Committee threw up radical possibilities and even
regionalism was considered on the model of the wartime organisation
of central government and along the lines of such academic critics
as Robson and Cole. It soon became obvious that the real need was
to provide services for the people and that this could not wait for
major structural reform which would meet vigorous opposition. The
short-run solution for dealing with those services which were not
within the capacity of the local units was increasing central control.

The Local Government Boundary Commission

The Local Government Boundary Commission was set up by the
coalition government under the Local Government (Boundary
Commission) Act, 1945. It was to make arrangements of boundaries as
between existing local authorities and it had the power to amalgamate
counties. It did not have a mandate to develop a new system and there
was no mention of the redistribution of functions between different
tiers. During the course of the Second Reading debate on the Bill,
there was only one critical speech. This was by John Silkin, later
to become Minister of Town and Country Planning. For him this was
a 'poor, timid, inadequate measure'.[7] He criticised precisely the point
that the Bill sought to improve the structure of local government
while in no way questioning the principles upon which the present
structure was based. Other than this speech there was almost complete
agreement upon the way in which the Commission was set up. There
was no division.

The Commissioners were appointed in 1945. The chairman,
Sir Malcolm Trustran Eve, Bart., was a barrister who had been
Chairman of the Rating and Valuation Association and of many other
public and quasi-public bodies including such organisations as the
Building Training and Apprenticeship Committee and the Air
Transport Licensing Board. He had a wide experience of the way in

which enquiries of this sort operated, but he was not associated with any particular local government interest. The deputy chairman was Sir Evelyn John Maude who had been Permanent Secretary at the Ministry of Health from 1940 to 1945. Other members included Sir James Frederick Rees, an economic historian and the Principal of the University College of South Wales and Monmouthshire, Sir George Hammon Etherton, who had been Town Clerk of Portsmouth (1908-20) and Liverpool (1920-22) and County Clerk of Lancashire (1922-24).

The Commission started by holding a number of conferences around the country in which local authority representatives from one or more areas would meet with a Commissioner or with an Assistant Commissioner. These latter were officers recruited on to the staff of the Commission mainly from the ranks of senior local government officers. There were meetings with local government associations and any other body which had a point of view to put.

In its 1946 report published in April 1947 these activities were reported but there was no real hint of the disquiet about the limited mandate upon which the work was taking place. Only one suggestion was made which was in any way radical. It had been suggested by Manchester and Salford that in the areas of certain conurbations there might be a case for an urban county, not unlike the London County Council. The Commission considered this worthy of consideration.

During the course of 1947, it became clear to most of the Commissioners that their remit was too narrow. It would have been possible to adjust boundaries between existing local authorities but increasingly this appeared to be a second-best solution. A more radical solution was necessary, because the position of local government had changed so much since 1888. A thorough-going review was necessary, including a review of functions. The sought a discussion with the Minister of Health, Aneurin Bevan, and it was agreed with him that, in their next report, they could go outside their terms of reference. They could recommend that new legislation be brought in which would give them powers to carry out a much more radical review including a review of functions.[8]

In the course of their 1947 Report[9] this point is made:
We have come to the definite conclusion that 'effective and convenient units of local government administration' cannot everywhere be procured without a fresh allocation of cunctions between the various types of local authorities.
and again
We have definitely reached the conclusion that in many areas – and these cover the great bulk of the population – our present powers and instructions do not permit the formation of local government

units as effective and convenient as in our opinion they should be
be . . . our experience confirms the statement made recently in
Parliament by the Minister of Health, 'Everyone who
knows about local government feels that it is nonsense to talk
about functions and boundaries separately. They have to be taken
together . . .'[10] We have no jurisdiction over functions.[11]

In view of this the Commission therefore made a number of far-reaching
recommendations:

Put in a sentence our principal recommendation was that the
middle-sized towns of the country should occupy an intermediate
position between county broughs and non-county boroughs,
and while forming part of the county for certain purposes
(police, fire and parts of town and country planning services)
should administer in addition to the ordinary functions of a non-
county borough, the services of education, health, the care of the
old and the disabled and parts of town and country planning.
We also recommend a new and more flexible system for deciding
in each county the delegation of functions from first-to second-
tier authorities and repeated our earlier recommendations for
an assimilation of the functions of the three types of the latter —
boroughs and urban and rural districts.[12]

In the case of the twenty largest towns or conurbations the
Commission suggested setting up a one-tier urban county along the
lines of the present county boroughs and it also recommended the
union of certain of the smaller counties such as Rutland with Leicester,
and Lincolnshire (Holland) with Lincolnshire (Kesteven). This was a
radical attempt to face the problems of local government. Especially
noteworthy was the proposal for an entirely new sort of unit and the
rearrangement of functions.

There were certain political straws in the wind which suggested
that the gentlemen in Westminster and Whitehall had their eyes on a
country-wide solution. It appeared that this might take a two-tier
form. These indications were, however, conflicting. The Minister
himself said at the 1946 AMC conference that there was to be no
'tearing up of the map'. Adjustments within the present system were
what were really required. Alderman Key, Parliamentary Secretary,
made the following statement to the West Midland Regional Labour
Conference:[13]

My conviction is that we have to make a new machine to do a new
job. Democracy cannot be served by outworn institutions, no
matter how much history is attached to them . . . We are not going
to get real planning in this country if we are going to separate the
planning of urban areas from rural areas . . . Let us have a two-tier
system of local Government — the big functions carried out by

regional authorities and the smaller functions by smaller authorities.

These contradictions were perplexing. Answering a Parliamentary question inviting him to explain this statement by his colleague, the Minister repeated that there was no intention of changing the local government system but Mr. Key's remarks were in line with a group within the Labour Party which had advocated the setting up of regional councils.

In order to get the full picture of political reaction to the Boundary Commission's report it is important to look at other sources.

The national papers virtually all commented favourably. *The Economist,* which for long maintained a high standard of critical analysis of local government, commented:

> This plan represents a fine achievement in the admixture of reforming zeal and political realism. Some drastic changes are involved but these are framed in a way that should cause the minimum of discontent among the existing local authorities and do the least possible harm to tradition and sentiment. The plan, therefore, has some chance of winning parliamentary acceptance. But this strength is also its weakness. While the proposed new system is undoubtedly an improvement it contains failings of its own which might become fatal with the passing of time.
> Their proposal is that the whole of England should be divided into 67 new counties none of which would have a lower population than 200,000.[14]

The Economist felt that this limit was too low. Another major problem was how to deal with the conurbations and here the Commission had not developed a clear policy.

No other national newspaper took up the plans in such detail. On the other hand, only the *Daily Graphic* was openly hostile. Its correspondent condemned 'the plan for the dismemberment of the living body of Britain'. The local press was often vigorously critical where it circulated in an area which faced demotion: but this was not an issue to hit the national headlines. Only the *New Statesman* commented upon the political forces which might affect the government's handling of the report. The county boroughs, it claimed, stood to lose most by the scheme. It was precisely in these areas that there were the highest concentrations of Labour supporters and therefore there would be vigorous opposition from within the party itself. The *New Statesman* recalled that, of all the policy documents prepared by the party during the war, that on local government reform was the one which caused the most heated dissent.

From the government itself, despite the public debate, there was no reaction to the report. In spite of a personal letter from Trustram Eve to Bevan no answer was forthcoming. Finally, with no warning, came a statement advising the House of Commons of the impending dissolution of the Commission.

> I am sure that the House will share the views of the Government that we are all very much indebted to the Local Government Boundary Commission under the able chairmanship of Sir Malcolm Trustram Eve for the very valuable reports which they have prepared and for the manner in which they have applied themselves to their duties. At the same time, the Commissioners are under the difficulty that the Local Government (Boundary Commission) Act, 1945, from which they derive their powers, limits their operations to the review and alteration of local government areas; they have no power to alter the structure of local government or to vary the function of different classes of authority. The Commission, in their annual reports, have drawn attention to the disadvantages of these limits. The White Paper on local government, published by the coalition government of January 1945 which recommended the setting up of the Local Government Boundary Commission recognised that the machinery for local government reorganisation might have to be changed with changes in circumstances – and the alterations to the functions of local authorities effected since the Act of 1945 have undoubtedly changed the position. The government have come to the conclusion that, in present conditions, it is difficult for the Commission to proceed with its work and they have decided to repeal the Act of 1945 which will involve the winding up of the Commission.[15]

In order to understand this reaction and indeed the attitude of the Minister to the whole question it is necessary to look at the background of other events. Bevan was, as Minister of Health, deeply involved in the establishment of the National Health Service. This was a major undertaking which took up a great deal of his time. It also involved a great deal of emotional commitment on Bevan's part in the sense that the health of the nation, and especially of the working classes, had an immense symbolic importance. Thus, the setting up of the Health Service took up both time and emotional energy. Secondly, Bevan had little experience of or interest in local government. He had very few sympathetic dealings with those members of the government like Chuter Ede, Morrison or Tomlinson who were involved in local government. Thirdly, it is important to remember that these politicians just mentioned *were* in the government. They had been brought up in local government and had deep commitments to it: Morrison to London, for example, and Chuter Ede to county government. With the Cabinet constituted as it was there seemed little possibility of getting through a measure of reform which was as thorough-going as that in the report of the Local Government Boundary Commission. Immediately after the war a number of alternative schemes for structural reform had been prepared by officials in the Ministry of Health but Bevan had shown no interest at all. When the Commission report came through there was a general consensus among the officials that the time was inopportune, given the make-up of the Cabinet and the importance of the post-war plans. The proposals were allowed to drop.

This development seems predictable. It had been decided, before the Commission was appointed, that there was to be no large change. The exigencies of the post-war situation were such as to ensure that this decision would be maintained. The Local Government Boundary Commission simply did not have the authority to demand the reversal of a decision of this kind.

In introducing the Second Reading debate on the Local Government Boundary Commission (Dissolution) Bill, the Parliamentary Under-Secretary to the Minstry of Health, Arthur Blenkinsop, made it clear that the government had decided against even modest changes.

When my Right Honourable Friend announced the Government's intention of winding up the Boundary Commission he said that the repeal of the Local Government Boundary Commission Act would restore the position substantially to what it was before the passing of the Act until such time as the Government have had an opportunity of reviewing the structure and functions of local government. This review is now taking place . . .[16]

There is no evidence that any review of this nature was ever taken up seriously and one must assume that the announcement of its existence was a way of holding up the most limited changes. Blenkinsop's reference to 'the position . . . (as) it was before the passing of the Act' meant that any alteration of boundaries would have to take place on the passing of a Private Act. This was and is an extremely expensive procedure. For practical purposes it was putting an almost impossible barrier in the way of adjustment.

The Lean Years

In the years between 1949 and 1954 there was little initiative from the government for reform. Instead, there was an attempt to make the existing system work more tolerably. One effect of post-war conditions was to increase control by departments over local authorities. Many councils complained about this until in January 1949, when reorganisation seemed no longer possible, the Local Government Manpower Committee was set up. It gathered representatives of both sides . . .

To review and co-ordinate the existing arrangements for ensuring economy in the use of manpower by local authorities and by those government departments which are concerned with local government matters — and to examine in particular the distribution of functions between Central and Local Government and the possibility of relaxing departmental supervision of local authority actactivities and delegating more responsibility to local authorities.[17]

The date of appointment is significant. Within its limited terms of reference it was successful and many of its suggestions for relaxing control were accepted.

Winds of Change

In October 1954 Duncan Sandys became Minister of Housing and Local Government. On 17 November the first of a series of meetings were held, at the invitation of the Minister, to iron the whole question out. The difference was that there was now a Minister who was personally interested in the subject. Sandys[1] solution to the intransigent attitude of the different sides was a conference which would last for several days. His technique of getting argreement was to set all those concerned around a table and keep them there, if necessary, for a very long time indeed, until some sort of agreement had been reached. At other times Sandys used this technique with great success: on Rhodesia to accept the 1961 Constitution and on the leaders of the British aircraft industry. Within the limits which he himself recognised and drew, it worked.

At the first meeting he made it clear that there could be *no radical change in the structure of local government.* No type of local authority was to disappear. Thus it became relatively easy to reach a limited aim. The initial point of the meetings was to establish what were the differences between the associations and to find a way round them.

On the important subject of the conurbations it was agreed that the provincial ones would be dealt with in the same review as the rest of the country. Each conurbation would be looked at as a whole and the effect of changes on the whole district would be taken into account. Initially it was also agreed that there should be a minimum population in order to apply for county borough status but there should be a difference between applications from authorities within a conurbation and those outside. Soon after the joint meeting it was understood that the Ministry foresaw Canterbury as the only candidate for demotion and they were not in favour of any minimum population figure to be regarded as a *sine qua non* of promotion. Instead all boroughs of approximately 100,000 inhabitants would be regarded *a priori* as fit candidates while those under that figure would have to make upt a special case.

With regard to authorities in the London area the agreement was different. London was to have special treatment – probably a Royal Commission: and Middlesex was to remain two-tier. This was to cause a lot of activity on the part of the Middlesex boroughs.

In terms of the general principles of local government it was agreed that an easier method of changing boundaries was required and that a Commission should be set up. It should take into account the effect of boundary changes on the whole of the surrounding area. It was also agreed that the county districts should have more power.

On 22 March Mr. Sandys was able to announce to the House that agreement had been reached between the local government associations[18] and himself on future plans for the system. This agreement was limited to a modification of the existing system and it was, moreover, restricted to structure rather than to functions or finance.

In August 1956 the White Paper *Area and Status of Local Authorities in England and Wales*[19] appeared. It was to be the first of three; the other two were to deal with functions and finance. It pointed out the disadvantages in terms of speed and expense of the private Bill procedure. A new machinery for review was obviously necessary and this was to be in the Commission. After this Commission had reported there was to be a standstill for a period; fifteen years had been suggested. While there was no need for a massive change in the structure it was certainly clear that larger units were needed both in the conurbations and elsewhere and there was a need to reduce the number of unduly small county districts. It was suggested that within the conurbations county boroughs should have a population of at least 125,000. Outside the figure was to be 100,000. On the structure of government within the conurbations, the Commission was to be given a free hand.

The achievement of this White Paper and the following should not be underestimated. They were limited in their scope but they represented agreement between the town and the county sides which at one time seemed impossible. It had needed a Minister who was prepared to dedicate himself to the the task of reform.

As yeat the subject of local government finance had not been touched. In February, however, during a debate in the Commons, the government made a statement on the subject to the effect that the arrangements for local government finance were to be changed by replacing more of the percentage grants by a General Grant. The apparent aim was to give local authorities more freedom in their use of funds. They would, it was claimed, be able to spend the money from such a grant without restriction as to particular services. To some extent, both the arguments for and against the General Grant were misleading. The main controls which ministries have over the performance of local authorities are not financial but administrative through regulations, circulars and Administrative Memoranda and through informal contacts between the officers of the ministry concerned and those of the local authority.

It is impossible to understand this change in local authority finance without taking the national economic position into account. This was a time of severe economic difficulty for Britain. The Conservative government of the day was taking steps to curb public expenditure and local government would certainly be included in this scaling-down. In February of 1956 the Chancellor (Mr. Macmillan) had imposed hire purchase controls and had cut public investment. In December over £200 million had been drawn from the IMF and a standby credit of £264 million arranged. In September of the next year (1957) the situation had become so bad that Bank Rate was raised from 5 per cent to 7 per cent and a ceiling of £1,500 million was imposed on public sector capital spending. When one considers that local government expenditure is a major part of public expenditure as a whole, it is quite clear that the Treasury could not hope to maintain control of the economy without controlling the spending of local authorities. Under the old percentage grant scheme, this control was weaker since local authorities, by undertaking a project, could put great pressure on government for financial support amounting to a fixed percentage of the total cost. By means of general grants, the government could decide in advance what the allocation to any authority was to be and it could not be moved from this.

Finally in May 1957 the White Papers on finance and functions appeared.[20] The government was in favour of more responsibility going to the lower-tier authorities, especially in the case of 'personal' services such as the domiciliary health services, children's services, and education. Authorities with a population of over 60,000 should be entrusted with most local government services. Under the population limit of 60,000 these powers could be exercised if the Minister was satisfied by the authority that it could be efficient.

The 1958 Act

The major points in the 1958 Local Government Bill were first, the introduction of a general grant in place of the existing percentage grants for specific services, the setting up of Local Government Commissions for England and Wales to review the boundaries and other arrangements and the re-rating of industry. Part III of the Bill referred to functions but there was to be no redistribution. It will later be shown that this was because of the difficulty of getting agreement from the associations. In view of this it was decided to deal with the question on a service by service basis.

The Bill started its progress through the Commons in November 1957. Although there had been intense lobbying by all sorts of interests between the White Paper and this stage, little of it raised serious questions about structural reorganisation. The burden of the debate on the Second Reading[21] and in Standing Committee was concerned with the financial aspects. The Labour Opposition argued, as it had during the debate on the White Papers, that these clauses of the Bill, far from giving local authorities freedom from central control were really aimed at redistributing local authority expenditure;[22] that education and health services would suffer since a General Grant did not encourage local authorities to do more as percentage grants had. On the contrary, local authorities would be given a fixed sum of money out of which all their expenses had to be found. There was no way of getting more help from central government as a result of increased local effort. The main Opposition spokesman on local government, Michael Stewart, made the point that, if percentage grants were bondage for local authorities, it was peculiar that local authorities associations had not complained about them. In the forty years of percentage grants there had been little comment by the associations.

There seems little doubt that the General or Block grant was aimed at economy in local government expenditure rather than at greater local freedom. The White Paper on finance had described the percentage system as an 'indiscriminate incentive to further expenditure'[23] and at the Conservative Party Conference, the Financial Secretary to the Treasury, Enoch Powell, described Block Grant as part of the government's machinery to check inflation. These comments have to be understood against the background of the economic crisis which was going on at the time and which led to a financial squeeze in 1958. A stringent examination of the local authority budget was introduced. This was aimed at cutting out all superfluous items. Far from giving local government more autonomy, this new type of grant meant less freedom. All the old administrative controls of central government existed, and in addition, where specific grants were automatic and could be increased by local authority initiative, the new grant had now to be debated and approved by Parliament every two years. Much more was now left to Ministerial initiative. In addition the government increased its power of approval over capital loans.

The 'Sandys' negotiations and the Bill of 1958 therefore set up a Commission which would adjust the boundaries of local authorities within the existing structure. Much of the rhetoric of the debate was conducted in terms of giving more power to the local authorities. The financial arrangements reveal, however, that this was not a substantive aim of the government, however important a symbol it may have been. The major concern was to improve the efficiency of the local authorities in the performance of their services.

The Local Government Commission

The instructions given to the new Commission[24] were carefully considered by all the interested parties before they were issued. The Commissioners had to consider nine factors. First, they were to take into account not only the efficiency of the one authority whose boundaries they were considering but also the effect of the changes on the workings of the whole area; and improvement to a county borough's efficiency might leave the surrounding counties and other authorities complete emasculated. Secondly, the Commissioners were to consider the degree to which community of interest could be said to exist between the authority seeking extension and the area claimed. It was to be expected that, if a county borough claimed an extension which would take in a village or even a non-county borough with its own community traditions, this would be disallowed by the Commissioners. It was not only the present situation which was to be taken into account but the economic and industrial characters of the two or more areas, they physical features, the size and shape of the areas, the records of administration in all relevant areas, their financial resources and, finally, the wishes of the populations. All of these considerations were capable of very conservative interpretation indeed and we shall see that the Commission interpreted them to allow only limited changes in the first stages of their work. It was only later that they seemed to give full weight to another directive which urged that they should take note of any development or expected development in the area as well as of the existing situation. Added to all this was the stipulation that a population of 100,000 either already existed or expected in the near future was a necessary condition for the creation of a new county borough. The whole tenor of the regulations was against a forward-looking interpretation.

It has already been noted that there were parts of the regulations which could have a different interpretation. In situations where it was obvious that boundaries were wrong the Commission could impose a radically different solution. One such procedure was built into the distinction between Special and General Review areas. In the latter, which accounted for most of the land area of the country, the

Commission was confined to reviewing the arrangements of the top-tier authorities. In these areas more or less conventional changes would be applicable. County boroughs might be extended and boundaries in general would be adjusted within the existing system. The adjustment of boundaries in the second tier would be left to the counties. In the Special Review Areas however, the great conurbations, more extensive solutions were possible. Since it was necessary to consider the areas as a whole, the Commission had full powers to consider and recommend new arrangements for all tiers. Moreover they could step outside the existing system to recommend new types of authority such as a continuous county borough (a one-tier authority covering a very large land area) or a continuous county.

George Jones points out that in their early reports the Commission was hesitant about how it should proceed.[25] In one of its first report there are a few paragraphs which show how the Commissioners then saw their tasks.

> To be effective, in our judgement, an authority must be able to provide for itself comprehensive services of a high quality over the whole range of its functions. It is not enough that an authority is able to provide the minimum requirements imposed by statute or regulation, it must have the capacity to go beyond those minimum requirements to develop new aspects of services and of technical change. An effective local authority should and would be capable of meeting any new demand made upon it and adapting itself to the changing conditions with which it is likely to be faced.[26]

This could have meant the use of sweeping changes to make the whole system more effective. The reference to beating new paths did not leave much hope for the smaller authorities who often operated on 'minimum requirements'. The Commission was required to arrange for 'convenient' as well as efficient local government. The interpretation of 'convenience' often seemed to give the smaller authorities more hope. The Minister required the Commission to have regard to the number, size, shape and boundaries of the local authorities within a review area, the travelling facilities within and between them, their effect on local services and on the access of council members and the public to the local administrative areas. Here the emphasis seems to be on smaller size as a balance to the economies of scale which might have been considered to render the authority more effective.

In virtually every case the Commission which made the preliminary investigations seemed to be most interested in the case loads borne by each of the local authority services which gave small authorities like Cambridgeshire, Ely and Rutland some concern. These, indeed, were the authorities for which reorganisation was proposed. On the other hand, the Commission gave itself lots of room to accept anomalies of size and arrangement by saying:

The Act itself requires us to consider the convenience of local authorities' areas. This means the need to have authorities that are reasonably 'local', that is accessible geographically and responsible to local needs and feelings. Most people think if this in terms of authorities that are not too big, not too far away and made up of elements that are not too diverse. It is clear to us in our examination of a number of counties that although they are of different size and make-up there is no one prescription for convenience. There are many different ways in which counties seem to us to achieve satisfactory local government County government is, moreover, in the rural areas a three-tier structure, with the districts and parishes supplying a valuable local foundation.[27]

These general attitudes seemed to direct the Commission towards grudging modifications of the present system. Given that the whole dynamic of change came from the expansion of the towns, and especially the county boroughs, it looked as if the full weight of the new demand was to be ignored. As Jones points out, the specific instructions to the Commission on the subject of county borough expansion emphasised this point. Paragraph II of the Local Government Commission's Regulations (1958) required that it must consider whether an area, to which a county borough lays claim, is not only 'substantially a continuation of the town area' but also if it has 'closer and more special links' with the county borough than 'those which necessarily arise from mere proximity'. Jones points out that the Commission had to reconsider

whether land not yet built up would, if a development plan were carried out in the future, be a continuation of the town area, and finally it is to consider whether there would be a balance of advantage in any change to the inhabitants of the county borough and the county district, and its effect on the organisation of the county and the county districts remaining within it.[28]

As the author remarks: 'the implications of these instructions is that the burden of proof lies with the county borough to justify its claim for expansion.'[29]

With all their balancing of claims it is not in doubt that there was a leaning towards the preservation of the existing system. It was most likely then that the Commission's reports would appear to favour the counties and the two-tier system in general. As Jones points out, the first reports of the Commission were in this direction. County boroughs had to make out a very special case for extensions to be recommended. Whereas the AMC had been on record since the war as being in favour

of a 'city region' approach, the Commission in its East Midland
General Review Area report specifically rejected this alternative.

Jones illustrates this orientation of the Commission by working
through the initial four final reports. He analyses the arguments used
by both sides and points out that the Commission concluded that
Regulation II prevented it from allowing annexations of built-up
land to county boroughs except under very special circumstances.
Continuity of development was not considered sufficient on its own.
Where the areas to be annexed were large municipal boroughs
which had grown separately from the county borough, where
development was not on a wide front (as in ribbon development)
or was broken by even a small strip of rural land, the proposed
annexation was disallowed. The Commission also rejected
claims to areas which were essentially parts of the county
boroughs in terms of continuous development on a wide front, if this
injured the capacity of the adjoining county to provide efficient
services. This attitude set the seal on the Commission's acceptance of
the existing system. Many spokesmen of the towns pointed out that
this bolstering up of county government strengthened an already weak
system. Nevertheless it is important to notice that, from the
beginning, the Commission accepted the point of view of the White
Paper that county borough government was the normal form of
government for large towns. This was a point made specifically by
the Vice-Chairman of the Commission, Michael Rowe, QC, in his
opening speech in Cambridge.[30]

Around this time various other events occurred which
affected the work of the local Government Commission and,
indeed, local government as a whole. These events were the
publication of the Buchanan Report, the South East study and
the report of the Royal Commission for local government in
Greater London.[31]

Reform of London Government

There had been several attempts to reform London's government.
The reasons for change are simply stated. The movement of
population and business had been such that the boundaries of the
London County Council meant very little in terms of the area
where Londoners lived. The situation in this respect was worse
than anywhere else in Britain simply because of the drawing power
of the metropolis. The result was that, outside the core of the LCC, the
area of London was controlled by three county boroughs,
Croydon, East Ham and West Ham, five Counties, Surrey, Kent,
Essex, Hertfordshire and Middlesex, and many urban districts. To make

things worse, relationships between the authorities were not always good.

Since 1899, when the London Government Act was passed, the pattern of administration in the metropolis had been different from that in the rest of the country. Not only is London the capital, but its size and its prospects for yet more growth makes it a candidate for different treatment. From 1888 there had been an upper-tier urban 'county' and a second tier composed wholly of boroughs. The distribution of functions between the tiers is different from the usual one.

The first point about the Herbert Commission was that it was an examination of a conurbation with the probable conclusion that the administrative area should be enlarged. Such a study led the way to change in other areas. The move to a larger scale of operation was in the air.

The Commission recommended that the boundaries of London be extended in such a way as to take in the old LCC area and to add to it the whole of Middlesex, large parts of Surrey, Kent and Essex and part of Hertfordshire. All this should be consolidated in the Greater London Council Area and, in addition, the three county boroughs, Croydon, East Ham and West Ham should lose their first-tier status. The Greater London Council should have responsibility for planning and traffic management and general educational policy in the whole of the area while the second-tier Greater London Boroughs, with a minimum of 100,000 population apiece, would administer other functions. After a bitter struggle[32] the main outline of these recommendations was accepted. As a result of pressure from the London teachers a separate education authority was set up for Inner London covering the old LCC area. Since the outer boroughs would, therefore, be education authorities on their own, the government felt it necessary to increase their minimum size to 200,000. The London Government Bill finally became law on 31 July 1963.

It is important to see the reform of London government in the context of local government reform as a whole. The dates indicate the decisions on London were being taken at precisely the same time as the rest of the country was being considered. The Royal Commission was set up on 29 July 1957 at the time when discussions were under way about the Local Government Act, finally passed in 1958. The new system was inaugurated in 1963 when the Local Government Commission was hard at work. It was impossible, therefore, that the work in London would not be taken into account. First of all, there was a clear move not just towards the adjustment of boundaries but to amalgamations on a large scale. The second point was that functions were rearranged. In particular there was a recognition of the role of planning and traffic management and the need that they should be exercised over the very largest area. London government reform was politically easy because it was perceived by the party in government, the Conservatives, to be in their political interest. The inclusion of the outer suburbs could mean that Labour's long-standing control of the LCC could be broken. There was a political impetus behind the measure which was lacking in general local government reform.

The South East Study

The South East Study faced the problem of population drift. In spite of earlier predictions it seemed realistic to assume that Britain's population was on the increase. Moreover, in spite of efforts like the new towns policy and attempts to regulate the location of industry, more and more people were coming to live in the South East.

There are expected to be at least three and a half million people living in South Eastern England by 1981; it might prove to be more . . . This report explains why such a large increase should be planned for and suggests various ways in which the planning of it could be done.[33]

The study was undertaken by officials of the Ministry of Housing and Local Government which itself was significant. It meant that a central government department was, for the first time, taking a direct hand in physical planning. A strategy was laid down. The second point is the belief that something *could* be done about it. Something could be done about the need to overspill about one million Londoners in the twenty years between 1961 and 1981 and something could be done about the acute land problem around London caused not only by the population growth but also by the fact that London and the surrounding area had a high rate of employment growth. The heart of the problem was that, although there was congestion in the region as a whole 'from the east to Dorset' it was particularly bad in London itself and in the outer metropolitan region. Something had to be done to redistribute population within this region.

It was recommended that:

There should be a second generation of new and extended towns, conceived on a larger scale, than those now being built. The need is for big schemes in locations favourable for growth. They should be accommodating London overspill and should attract some of the immigrant population and employment growth that might otherwise be drawn in the London orbit. The biggest of these schemes, should in time, grow into major cities of the future, and act as strong counter-attractions to London. A programme for one to one and a quarter million people is required.[34]

To accomplish this three new major cities were envisaged: Southampton-Portsmouth, Bletchley and Newbury and in addition several new or expanded towns.

One point already referred to in Chapter 3 is that physical planning and economic planning were integrated in this report. It was impossible to understand the physical problems of congestion without realising the economic thrust behind the inflow of population. In the same way economic measures had to be taken in conjunction with physical planning to relieve the problem.

Central government was beginning to involve itself in a new field of regional economic and social development which was bound to cross-cut the activities of local authorities. Other studies, such as those of the underdeveloped regions, the North East, and Central Scotland also pointed in this direction. Town and country planning was bound to be affected by this new foray of the state but it would be difficult not to find a local authority service in which there would be no repercussions. Once more the world of local government was given warning that a massive new move on the part of the centre was taking place.

The fact of the matter was that only central government could deal with the problem. The scale of approach was regional and local authorities were not capable of tackling it. Time and again co-operation for planning purposes had been a failure. The failure of local government to deal with what was a fundamental problem meant that its usefulness was called in question. The trend to regional thinking for local government was reinforced.

It is also worth noticing that it was about this point that the Commission itself began to reconsider its position. Jones points out the paragraphs in which they draw attention to the movement of young and middle-class people from the centres of large towns to their fringes. This was seen as a definite threat to the pool of potential councillors and to those capable of occupying leading positions in the county boroughs. Social considerations were now recognised as being crucial.[35]

The Buchanan Report

Finally, the publication of the Buchanan Report *Traffic in Towns*[36] and its impact on local government thinking must be discussed. Once again the Commission was conscious of this development.

The report was written by Mr. Colin Buchanan who was at that time a civil servant in the Ministry of Transport. In 1960 the Minister, Ernest Marples, invited him to draw together a working group from

among his colleagues. In addition, a "Steering Group" was formed
under Sir Geoffrey Crowther. It consisted of private individuals who
would be able to draw policy conclusions from the study more
freely than a civil servant might feel proper.

The report was different from previous traffic studies in that it was
concerned, not simply with the movement of motor traffic but with
the interaction between motor traffic and the environment. Buchanan
pointed out that the motor car was likely to become more and more
widely used and owned in Great Britain. Its comparable advantage
was that it provided a flexibility and 'door to door' service which
other forms could not give. On the other hand there were disadvantages
in that the motor car destroyed amenities. Its very usefulness brought
a popularity and with the popularity a congestion which destroyed its
convenience. It was often impossible to go from door to door because
other cars might already be parked there. There were problems of
noise and fumes. There were problems of parking and garaging. There
was the ever-present problem of accidents. The motor car also led to
particular sorts of physical development. Its flexibility meant
that car owners could travel long distances to and from work. Even
villages which were quite separated from the towns became urban
dormitories. As far as the towns were concerned, the cause of the
problem was that their layout was not suited to the motor car. For a
car to develop its potentiality there had to be long runs in city streets.
In most cities cross streets broke up this long run. Secondly, the cities
were not designed for the avalanche of cars which came into them each
morning. There had to be a vigorous attempt at traffic management
and at the designing of towns to cope with the motor cars.

Buchanan made a number of suggestions for development and
traffic management. The drift of the report was towards the
management of traffic over wide area so that flows could be
canalised and controlled before they got to a torrential stage at the
city boundary. The point had already been met in the Herbert
recommendation for Greater London which gave traffic
management to the GLC. It was obvious that this new service
was going to be of importance elsewhere. The real implications
for local government were more clearly picked out by the report
of the steering rgoup. The recommended that each urban region
should have a 'regional development agency'. This was to be
organised on business lines acting through a General Manager on the
model of the New Town Corporation.

The agency should have the necessary powers to co-ordinate
the planning for all local authorities in the area . . . where nobody
would take the initiative, the Agency should be empowered to act
itself. And to enable it to do so, it should be the channel through

which all grants of Treasury money for any purpose connected with development should flow.[37]

For many local authorities the message was clear. The report pointed to the inter-related planning of town centre and periphery. It made a strong case for the inclusion of peripheral areas into the towns. It also raised the question of whether there was any point in setting up any local authorities other than those which operated over a large area.

There were other events which had an effect on local government thinking. At least two Acts had had a centralising effect. The Water Resources Act arranged a grouping of authorities for water undertakings. Similarly, the Police Act 1964 laid down the ground work for amalgamations of forces. Local government was being forced to come together into larger units whether it liked it or not. Government was committed to a form of central intervention threatening the structure of local authorities rather in the fashion of the wartime Regional Commissioners. Sir Keith Joseph, the Minister of Housing and Local Government, launched a scheme of regional authorities. On the suggestion of the Ministry, Joseph addressed a meeting of the Royal Institute of Public Administration on 15 April 1964 where he rejected any possibility of these authorities taking over the job of local government. They were to be extensions of central government to deal with regional development and the relief of unemployment. It was no surprise that when Labour came to power late that year it should be forced to think about major local changes.

The Maud Commission and the Movement to Reform

It was during the 1966-70 Labour government that serious moves towards reform were made. When one considers the obstructions of the 1940s and 1950s it is surprising to see the system so near to fundamental change.

There are a number of themes which may be summarised here. There was the effect of other political events which seemed to 'suggest' a system of local administration which was different from the present one. There was a movement towards running services on a larger scale than was possible within the existing local authority boundaries and this certainly had an effect upon thinking about local government structure. Secondly, and partly depending on this, there came a spate of articles and pamphlets which drew attention to the urgency of reorganisation. They were encouraged in this by the fact that a 'reform oriented' Labour government was now in office. Finally, the feeling that there was a need for reform was exacerbated by the obstruction of the Local Government Commissioners' work.

The Labour government came into office with a clear commitment
to efficiency and reform. As far as local government reform itself was
concerned there were no undertakings. Indeed, we shall see that it took
some time to persuade the Minister responsible that such moves were
possible. Nevertheless, the whole ethos of the administration was in the
direction of clearing away old things which were dilapidated or which
depended only on tradition for their justification. The previous
Conservative administration under Sir Alec Douglas-Home had not
given an impression of being at home with modern economic and
technological problems. The Labour Party, on the other hand, made
a considerable effort to prepare its leaders for coping with such a
concern. Many of the themes which were later picked up by Labour
had been developed by previous Conservative Ministers. Sir Keith
Joseph, we have seen, had gone into the possibility of a type of regional
administration.

When Labour came into office they were cautious. At the Labour
Party local government conference in April 1965, for example, the
Minister, R.H.S. Crossman, said:

> only practical reforms are likely to come from the
> recommendations of the Local Government Commission...
> the possibility of changing the Commission's terms of
> reference is a long way ahead.

And a few weeks later at the conference of the Town Planning Institute
he said, 'the idea of radical reform of local government is, in terms of
practical politics, a non-starter.'[38] Finally, speaking at the annual
meeting of the County Councils Association, he said, 'we have to work
on the assumption that the County Councils and the County Borough
Councils are always going to be with us.'[39] He spoke about the
necessity for ending the 'cold war' between them.

Nevertheless, in Crossman, the Department of Housing and Local
Government had one of the most radical and able Ministers in the
government. On the staff of the Ministry the Permanent Secretary,
Dame Evelyn Sharp, shared Crossman's attitude to local government
reform. It was significant that she had interested herself in the planning
work of this Ministry leaving the housing side to her colleague J.D. Jones.
Dame Evelyn was known to be a lady of definite views, one of which
appeared to be a suspicion of the capacities of smaller local authorities.
After she left the Ministry she expressed this personally on several
occasions. For example, in April 1962, speaking in Bristol she said:

> Part of the trouble in getting enough good people to serve arises
> from the fact that the areas and status of local authorities are
> often today too cramped or too small to enable a satisfactory
> job to be done.[40]

It is evidence of her desire for reorganisation that Crossman put her on on the Commission. She had been one of the few Whitehall people who had been prepared to face this.

The Buchanan Report, the South East Study, Development Area policy all had had some effect on government thinking before the 1964 election. Labour came into power committed to the exercise of economic planning. The most important member of the Parliamentary Party after the Prime Minister was placed in charge of a new Department of Economic Affairs and a National Plan was drawn up. At a sub-national level arrangements were made for economic planning and Regional Economic Boards and Councils were set up. The former were made up of civil servants seconded from their departments to deal with the affairs of that particular region. The Councils were made up of representatives of the local authorities, industry, the universities and other aspects of the life of the region. They were given the job of encouraging local enterprise and preparing a development plan for the region. Members were appointed by the Minister which caused criticism from the local government associations. For some time it was felt that this was the beginning of an attempt to replace local government. It certainly encouraged thinking in regional terms — a realisation that there were ways of dealing with local problems other than by local government in its traditional boundaries.

Economic planning was, of course, a function which local authorities did not traditionally tackle. In many other fields of local authority concern, however, there were changes in the direction of regionalism. In 1962 the Royal Commission on the Police had reported.[41] Only one member (Professor Goodhart) recommended the adoption of a national force but all agreed that many forces were too small. The optimum size was around 500 men and this entailed a population of around 250,000. The Police Act 1964 strengthened the power of the Home Secretary to amalgamate forces. In the years between the passing of the Act and 1970 the numbers of police authorities had thus been reduced considerably. A very old local authority service was now being run on a 'regional' basis.

Transportation was another area which had implications for structure. Many urban authorities had municipal transport undertakings, the scale of which had been made inadequate by modern developments. People commonly travelled to homes well outside the city boundaries and this, added to growing financial problems of municipal bus companies, led the government to set up Passenger Transport Authorities.

In May 1964 Sir Keith Joseph had established the Planning Advisory Group to work in co-operation with his Ministry. It was made up of Ministry officials, local government officers and private consultants and its job was 'to provide practical and expert advice' for local authorities in the field of planning. It was 'to assist in studying the implications for the techniques, procedures, and machinery of town and country planning of major developments that lie ahead in the planning field.' It was this philosophy which lay behind the setting up of Joint Planning Teams. The first, in 1968, covered the South East and others subsequently the North East and the North and eventually the whole country, region by region. The teams were made up of local government planning officers but the initiative came from the Ministry. It was they who were to work out physical plans for the regions.

All these developments in local government services helped to create a climate in which structural change seemed to be a possibility. In many cases there were *ad hoc* arrangements which changed the structure of local government for these particular services. In the 'sixties there were several services for which local authorities were deemed to be responsible but which were run by a series of committees or authorities in no way answerable to the electorate. These made up for the inadequacies of the existing structure but they were doing so in a way which might lead to more administrative confusion (if the experience of the nineteenth century was anything to go by) and which were potentially undemocratic.

Another development prepared the way for structural reform. The last Conservative government set up two committees chaired by Sir John Maud and Sir George Mallaby whose remit was respectively to look at the management and the staffing of local government.[42] These reported in 1967 and recommended a set of improvements which could be taken up by existing local authorities in order to improve their operations. It was recommended for example that committee systems should be streamlined to cut out committees which existed for reasons which were no longer valid or to amalgamate those which simply duplicated each other's work. Another of the many recommendations which were made was that there should be some sort of co-ordinating policy committee which would ensure that all parts of the local authority worked together. Those suggestions were made for the existing units. They did, however, help to create an atmosphere where past practice could be questioned.

This form of improvement might have been accommodated within units created by the Local Government Commission. There were important reasons why this soon appeared to be inadequate. At the beginning of its term of office it interpreted its remit in a conservative way. Although its later proposals were more radical, it could not recommend a wholesale change in local government and this was what many people were beginning to think of as the only

solution. The reason why they took this attitude had to do with the
other problem of the Local Government Commission. Even in its most
conservative proposals the Commission found itself bitterly opposed by
some local authority interest or other. There appeared to be no way in
which authorities were prepared to accept change for the good of the
system as a whole even if it meant the diminution of a few of their
own powers. On the contrary, local authorities who found that they
had lost even a small piece of territory almost inevitably went to the
furthest extremes to maintain themselves. It had not initially been
intended, for example, that parties could be represented by counsel.
Such was to become a common practice and made the work of the
Commission difficult. The local authorities were, in at least one
way, in a stronger position than the Commission for they knew the facts
of the local geography better than the Commissioners. They could
capitalise upon this when it became necessary to discuss the details
of boundaries. If the Commissioners were to make the slighest mistake
about local allegiances or the flow of traffic their whole scheme was
treated as if it had been invalidated. Thus the work of the
Commission went slowly. When Crossman did finally announce the
setting up of the Royal Commission one of the reasons mentioned
was the slowness of the Local Government Commission.

We have seen that Crossman took some time to be convinced that a
new device was necessary. Since he was a man conscious of the
intellectual currents of his time, it is fair to assume that he paid
some attention to the various pamphlets and articles which were
coming out and which recommended a more or less wholesale reform.
These came from supporters of both the large political parties.
J.L. Sharpe published a Fabian pamphlet[43] and there was also a
Bow Group publication,[44] both of which were critical of the small
units which made up the present system and suggested that plans
should be made to bring everything up to a bigger scale. The
pamphlets were also in agreement upon the ending of the town-
country division. On a different medium, the ABC television
programme *Power in Britain* picked up the same themes and
put them over to a wider audience. This activity created a public
atmosphere in which it seemed credible that a thorough reform of the
system should be tackled. It was not surprising when, at the
conference of the AMC in September 1965, Crossman announced
'a powerful and impartial committee as an essential first step towards
a radical reorganisation of local government'.

In February the appointment of a Royal Commission on Local
Government was announced 'to consider the structure of local
government in England, outside Greater London, in relation to its
existing functions; and to make recommendations for authorities

and boundaries and for functions and their division, having regard to the size and character of areas in which they can be most effectively exercised and the need to sustain a viable system of local democracy.' Such were the terms of reference in the Royal Warrant published on 31 May 1966. The Commission was to deal with the existing functions of local government only. There was controversy about whether authorities should take over the National Health Service as had been suggested when that service had been set up first of all but, for the present at any rate, there was no suggestion that any functions might be devolved to local government. More important, the Commission had no powers to consider the general devolution of power from Westminster, because a Royal Commission on the Constitution[45] was also set up with this topic as one of the most important terms of reference. It was not clear, however, when this latter Commission was set up, whether this would necessarily involve increasing the powers of local government as we know it. The second point to be noticed is that the Commission was to look at functions and boundaries but there was no mention about finance. When the establishment of the Commission was announced the Prime Minister explained that finance was not entirely excluded from the remit but that any real discussions of finance would have to wait for a government enquiry.[46] The Treasury would have a large say in any change of local government finance, since local authorities were such big spenders of government grants and other monies. In the debate before the 1958 Act there had been a similar situation. The government had been prepared to discuss the general principles of boundary revision with the local government associations but functions and finance were the subjects of separate White Papers which were not the result of negotiations outside the government. Finally, there were two considerations which the Commission had to bear in mind. First of all there was the effective exercise of services and secondly the maintenance of local democracy. These were to be the principles which were often in conflict.

In terms of the politics of the Commission, the membership is interesting. The chairman was Sir John Maud (later Lord Redcliffe Maud) who, when a don at Oxford, had written a well-known textbook about English local government.[47] In the civil service he had risen to be Permanent Secretary in the Ministry of Education. The Vice-Chairman was J.E. Bolton, Chairman of the Council of the British Institute of Management. Among the members were Dame Evelyn Sharp, who had just resigned as Permanent Secretary at the Ministry of Housing and Local Government, Victor Feather, the Deputy Secretary of the Trade Union Congress, Derek Senior, who at one time had been the extremely distinguished local government correspondent of the *Guardian* and Reginald Wallis, the North West Regional Organiser of the Labour Party. Although many of these Commissioners had known views on local government reform, they were not clearly linked with one or other side in the county-county borough struggle. There were others who had these connections. On the county side there was Peter Mursall, a member of the West Sussex County Council and John Longland, the Director of Education of Derbyshire. On the county borough side was A.H. Marshall, an ex-city Treasurer of Coventry, but, at the time of appointment the Associate Director of the Institute of Local Government Studies at Birmingham University, Dan Smith, an ex-leader of the Labour Group (and of the Council) in Newcastle-on-Tyne and Sir Francis Hill, an ex-Chairman of the AMC. It is clear from this listing that there was a balancing of the interests of the two 'sides' in local government. What is even more interesting is that these representatives worked together to produce a report which was quite different from the policies of their respective organisations, as though they had accepted that change was necessary and there had to be some compromise. All the Commissioners were advocates of quite thorough-going change. The presence of Senior alone would have meant this and in the first few weeks of the Commission's existence each member received a copy of his book *The Regional City,*[48] one of the most consistent plans for reform which had appeared. It was widely believed that Crossman had been impressed by this study. Certainly Crossman made it clear that the Commission was being set up to recommend a new approach to local government. In particular it was expected to recommend larger units and to get rid of the existing town-country dichotomy.

Events outside local government and subsequently inside local government made it both possible and necessary to think in terms of a new structure rather than an adjustment to the old one. Basic changes had taken place in the way in which people thought about physical planning. Where before it had been regarded as little more than an arrangement of uses of space within a given authority, now it was believed necessary to plan over an area much wider than most local authority territories and, in particular, the split between county borough and county no longer made any sense at all. Economic planning also meant that larger areas had to be thought about. In both these types of planning, the central government had moved towards larger units. One factor which should be taken into account is the use of planning as a profession. Immediately after the war, planners had come up through the staffs of local authorities, sometimes in the Engineers Department, sometimes in the Architect's. At the Annual Meeting of the Town Planning Institute in October 1969, the President pointed out that there had been 1,645 members in 1948 but in 1969 there were 4,168. In earlier times, planners had qualified with little more than the experience they gained within their own authorities; now there were over thirty courses at universities and other institutions.

Within local government itself, certain services were being run by authorities of a differenty type and scope from the traditional units. Finally, the arrival of a new government committed to a programme of reform laid the ground for a new appraoch and the personality of the relevant Minister was a crucial factor.

Several events took place while the Commission was sitting and which may have affected its thinking. One piece of evidence presented to Maud should be noticed: that of the ministries concerned with local government functions. It would be tedious to go into the differences between them largely because the differences concerned detail only. In broad outline the agreed. If one looks at the evidence of the Ministry of Housing and Local Government one comes upon reasoning very close to that discussed in Chapter 1.

The main shortcomings, in the Ministry's view, arose from the absence of a proper relationship between the structure of local government and the nature of the planning functions and planning problems to be tackled. This was more important than difficulties in the amalgamation of the various planning authorities and types of authority within the existing system.

Planning in local government has developed beyond the central and basic part of controlling land uses. It has to have regard to the need for the co-ordination of the main activities of the local government unit and their investment programmes to meet the evolving economic and social needs of communities much wider than those which existed in the nineteenth century when the present system of local government was established. In most parts the county's existing local planning authority when making provision for housing, employment, shopping, education, recreation and consequent traffic is often coping with demands and pressures arising not only in its own area but also from areas outside its boundaries. The decision of the planning authority which is taken in these circumstances inevitably impinges on the responsibilities and policies of its neighbours.[49]

In the Treasury evidence the implication of this form of structure was picked up. Local government expenditure had been growing very rapidly.

What is needed is a system of local government so geared that it cannot only handle effectively large and perhaps increasing expenditure and the financing of them but also obtain the best possible value for these expenditures.

To achieve this the objectives must be:
(a) to secure a structure of local government with units of
sufficient size to allow for efficient management and to command
the skills needed for efficient and economic control of the
services and the resources for which this was necessary.
(b) to secure that these authorities command sufficient
rateable resources to finance a large part of the cost of the services
they administer . . . At present many small authorities receive
sixty-five per cent to seventy per cent – in some cases more – of
their net income from government grants.
This would require a drastic reduction of the number of local
authorities and simplification of the financial structure of
local government.
This (i.e. financial efficiency) could be achieved by:
(a) establishing single authorities for each of the large
conurbations;
(b) combining into single authorities large free standing towns and
both the urban and the rural areas which surround them;
(c) organising the remaining county areas into the smallest number
of units which geographical considerations will allow.[50]

In order to implement these aims the Ministries recommended a series
of thirty to forty authorities to replace the counties, county boroughs
and county districts. The fact that all the departmental evidence pointed
so unanimously to unitary authorities and authorities of so large a scale
was an important reason for the Commission to go in this direction.

It was no surprise that, when the separate proposals for Welsh
re-organisation came along in July 1967 they considerably reduced
the number of authorities. Five new top-tier authorities replaced the
existing 13 and 164 districts were amalgamated into 36. It was clear
that the English Commission would have to be at least as radical.

In the same month there appeared a White Paper on planning
procedures.[51] The effect of this was to give local authorities a great
deal more autonomy by developing the idea of a Structure Plan.
This would be much more of an outline than that previously demanded
of the authorities for Ministry approval. Where before the Minister had
to decide on all sorts of minor local objections before the more
detailed plan was approved, now he merely had to looka t the broad
sweep. Minor objections were left to the local authority. This move
in the direction of freedom was also characteristic of the mood at
meetings of the Commission.

Up to now only events which have been in the direction of change
have been mentioned. The setting up of Department of Economic
Affairs marked a departure in intention from the traditional way in
which the country was managed. Many of the local authorities and

with them the AMC expressed grave fears that, with its talk of regions, this Ministry was poaching upon ground which was, by rights, the preserve of local authorities. In a very short time, the DEA was in trouble. The consequences were that the idea of a National Plan was scrapped and with it a great deal of the stress on regional planning. By the end of 1968 no regional plan had been produced and, when Professor Day of the London School of Economics resigned from the South Eastern Council he probably expressed the feelings of many members. It was, he said, 'a dreadful waste of time.'

These events must be considered as background to the work of the Commission. After a little over three years of discussion and hearing of evidence, the report was published in June 1969.

The Report of the Maud Commission

This was a turning point in the road to reform. It was not simply that Maud accepted most of the criticisms which had been made of the existing system. The Local Government Boundary Commission had eventually come round to this and had been sacked for its pains. In Maud's case, an official investigating body reported when the political circumstances were ripe for change. It was expected that the Maud Report would be radical and that the government would act upon it.

Which sort of radical reform should be followed? Maud made one set of recommendations[52] but there was a 275-page Memorandum of Dissent[53] by Mr. Derek Senior. Senior did not only suggest broad principles of reform counter to those of his colleagues. He specified boundaries and areas which put flesh upon the bones of his general principles. Clearly this was not a document which could be ignored. Moreover, it received support from an influential source. When Maud was set up there was also set up a Scottish equivalent, under the chairmanship of Lord Wheatley. Wheatley took longer to report than Maud but when, in September 1969, they did publish,[54] the conclusions of this Commission were much closer to Senior than they were to the views of the majority of the English commission.

The essential difference between Maud and Wheatley was the number of tiers which were recommended. Maud came down in favour of a one-tier system of sixty-one all-purpose authorities. In addition there would be eight provinces with councils elected by the members of the local authorities. These provincial councils would be planning bodies not responsible for the running of services and employing a very small staff. The Scottish Commission, and with it Mr. Senior, came down on the side of a two-tier system. The top tiers covered smaller areas than the provinces suggested by Maud but they had the responsibility for running the most important services. In the actual details of the services Wheatley and Senior were not identical. The differed in the scale of the areas which they chose but this was due to the facts of the geography of the two countries rather than with differences of principle. They agreed that local government services should be divided between two tiers of strata of councils. Even if it had not been for Senior's dissent it would have been essential for the government to consider the two-tier solution. Since Maud and Wheatley were set up at the same time it was inevitable that each should be read in the light of the other.

In place of the existing 1,200 local authorities, counties, county boroughs, non-county boroughs, urban districts and rural districts and the parishes, Maud recommended there should be sixty-one new local government authorities. Instead of the old pattern of different authorities for town and country there should be one type everywhere other than in certain 'metropolitan' areas. They would be centred upon an urban service centre but would take in a considerable area of countryside around. It would be wrong to think of a neat pattern with well-defined urban centres and clearly dependent rural surroundings. Instead the proposed local authorities contained one urban area which was the centre and several others which were subsidiary urban centres. In addition to this there was the surrounding rural area. An example will show what this means: Unit 29 was entitled Derby and Derbyshire. It included the existing county boroughs of Burton-upon-Trent and Derby and the boroughs of Buxton, Chesterfield and Ilkeston, not to mention a large number of urban districts. Thus, the main units of local government in England, instead of being purely rural or purely urban, were to be a mixture of the two. It is difficult to reduce the numbers of local authorities and at the same time give every small town together with its hinterland some independence. This appeared to be the plan which was put forward by the MAC and indeed it had an appealing simplicity. The actual proposal, however, meant that, for any authority, there was more than one, sometimes far more than one, urban centre, although most of the proposed authorities had one town which was larger and more important than any of the others.

The concept of the 'city region' dominated thinking about reorganisation. There are two kinds of city region. One relates to the area which surrounds a relatively small market town and which finds most of its services in such a centre. The second type relates to the area around a large town or metropolis and the provision of services which can only be found together in such large centres; an airport, major industry and so on. In making these proposals, Maud went in the direction of the second type of city region although he did not go so far as some witnesses, notably the government departments.

There were three exceptions to the proposed pattern of unitary authorities — the 'metropolitan regions' around Manchester, Liverpool, and Birmingham. In these areas a two-tier structure was recommended. A metropolitan authority would have responsibility for planning, transportation and major development and the metropolitan district councils would run education, personal social services, health and housing.

Maud suggested that the old organisation of local government should be scrapped and that in its place there should be a series of all-purpose authorities which would include urban areas and their rural hinterland. Maud's axe did not chop everything; he compromised a little:

> strict application of the principles of the city region would mean drawing a completely new local government map as if present boundaries did not exist, resulting in some very large areas in many parts of the country which would give no continuity with the past and to which we did not think people would be able to feel they belonged. The Ministry of Housing and Local Government advised us that the greater use of the new system made of present boundaries the easier would be the transition to it from the present system, but there was a more important point that we wished to preserve the historical strength of the existing local government system wherever possible and we were not persuaded that wholesale departure from present boundaries would be best.[55]

In addition to these unitary authorities, Maud proposed that there should be a system of local councils. These bodies were to be a way in which communities which had had representation through a council of their own in the unreformed system could be given a voice. To this extent they were a useful way of making towns and county boroughs *feel* that they were not be completely extinguished. The actual size of these local councils was undefined. They might be representative of old parish areas or towns. This aspect of the system would be determined by the extent to which local people felt themselves to be a local community in need of a council. The Commission did, however, have a clear idea of the job which the councils had to do:

> we do not see them as having statutory responsibility for any local government service . . . Their key function should be to focus opinion about anything that affects the well-being of each community and to bring it to bear on the responsible authorities: but they should have a number of powers to be exercised at discretion.[56]

All the powers of local councils should be concurrent powers, that is to say, powers which should also be possessed by the main authorities.[57]

The powers of local councils should relate first to the provision of amenities . . . and . . . those designed to promote local convenience.[58]

In other words these were to be not inconsiderable bodies. Maud emphasised that, since many of them would serve areas equivalent to present-day towns, they should not simply be heirs to the parishes but have extended powers; even including housing if they wished. As the Commissioners saw it, these councils were to stand outside the rest of the system. They would be much closer to the electors and could act as spokesman in a way that a bureaucratised local authority could not. Maud seemed to see this as a new departure for local government and, indeed, for British government. They were, of course, to have a general power to improve their area but it was central to Maud's concept that they should not be seen as bodies with power *over* their electorate. In as direct a way as possible they should be seen to express the will of the people.

Given that this was a new type of unit it is interesting to speculate why it appeared. The most obvious reason is that the Secretary of the National Association of Parish Councils, Charles Arnold-Baker, was a competent officer who prepared some of the best evidence that came before the Commission and made a good showing in his oral evidence. There was no question but that the Commission was impressed. One should also point out that the suggestion came at a time when it was politically convenient and socially appropriate. It was politically convenient because the proposed units were large. It made a great deal of sense to introduce councils which would operate at the level of smaller areas but which would not take away any of the powers from the other bodies. It was appropriate also in terms of the ideas of community politics and community participation which had become fashionable at that time. The general theme of participation was expressed in current thinking over the place of the worker in management. There was a reaction against the anonymity of the large cities and large housing estates.

The symbolic value of enshrining a community in this scheme of reform was high.

The Senior Version

In Chapter 1 of his memorandum Mr. Senior explained the differences of principle which lay between himself and his colleagues. They also sum up the differences between the English and Scottish Commissions. He bagan:

My colleagues take as their starting point the proposition that, in considering what changes are needed to remedy the ills we have

diagnosed (and agreed upon) there is one fundamental question —
namely, what size of authority or range of size, in terms of
population and of area is needed for the democratic and efficient
provision of particular services and for local government as a
whole. The answer they produce is expressed in terms of
population only: it takes no account of the geographical
requirements of democracy and efficiency.[59]

He pointed out that the majority of the Commissioners went on
to lay down the principle that 'to concentrate responsibility for all
main local government services in a single authority for each area
would help to make the idea of local self-government a reality.'[60]
In other words the main report took as an almost transcendent
principle the idea of a unitary authority. Senior did not quarrel with
the proposition that unitary organisation was a good to be sought.
He felt that it was not the only good and that when one actually
drew the boundaries of such unitary authorities, one found that,
in the majority of cases, the boundaries did not fit the facts of social
georgraphy. The main body of Commissioners 'perform the feat of
self-deception by taking population alone into account.' In a moment
we shall discuss instances where Senior tried to fault the other
Commissioners. Meanwhile we should notice that he made one
subsidiary but exceedingly telling point. The main report
interpreted the unitary principle to mean that 'units with populations
ranging from 250,000 to 1,000,000'[61] should be the local authorities.
There is no basis of evidence for the magic quality of this range.
Senior summed up the argument:

They have adopted a principle of organisation — the unitary
principle — and determined a range of population size for unitary
authorities by analysing the theroetical requirements of
functional efficiency and democratic viability in isolation from
the geographical context in which local government must operate . . .
I think the right approach is to start by analysing the facts of social
geography, the requirements of functional effectiveness and the
conditions of democratic viability in relation to one another,
to let the outcome of this analysis determine the appropriate scales
of units for groups of related functions, and then to see what
principle of organisation best fits the needs thus ascertained
and the practicalities of the transition to a new structure.[62]

Later he says:

As soon as one tries to apply this unitary principle to the
'realities of peoples' lives' in almost every part of modern
England one is confronted with a choice. One can create a series
of units based on coherent district communities in which case
one fragments planning and development problems and either

lets them go unsolved or violates the unitary principle by
superimposing a wider authority to deal with them. Or one can
create a single unit for the whole plannable area and deny the
district communities the right to democratic self-government
in the personal service field. But there is, of course, a third choice
worse than either; and that is to create units of intermediate scale
which suit neither kind of purpose and have no basis in
community structure.[63]

In accordance with these considerations Mr. Senior recommended a
mainly two-tier system of local government. The top tier was so
arranged to look after the major local government services: physical
planning, traffic management and passenger transport, water supply,
sewage, police, fire, education and several others. This was the regional
level. The district level was to look after the health service, personal
social services, consumer protection and 'all other functions involving
personal contact with the citizen.'[64] In addition to these two main
levels there should be a provincial level where the councils would be
responsible for long-term strategic planning and bringing the needs of
the province as a whole to the attention of the central government.
They were to be like the Provincial Councils of the main report in
having only a limited staff and no service responsibilities. There would
also have been a grass-roots level of community councils. Like the
regional and district councils at this level would have had a general
power but no statutory functions. Their main task would have
been to act as sounding boards for community feelings as in the main
report.

There is another general point which distinguished Maud and
Senior. Both claimed to be devotees of the 'city region' idea. The main
report recommended that the new boundaries stick fairly closely to
the old; but it is difficult to see how this could be achieved and the
principle of the city region retained. Senior made the point:

another of my colleagues' principles is that the areas of the new
units must be based upon the interdependence of town and
country — a proposition which I am, of course, in complete
agreement with. My objection here is that the principle
as stated does not go anything like far enough. It would be
satisfied if we merely recommended, as some witnesses suggested
we should, that the existing county boroughs be submerged in the
existing counties. But this would not take us five per cent of the
way towards creating a structure that would meet the functional
requirements of the environmental services. For nearly all the
present county boundaries entirely fail to recognise the only
kind of interdependence between town and country that is
relevant — namely the interdependence of a major urban centre

with that particular tract of country (including lesser urban centres) whose inhabitants find that particular centre more accessible than any other offering a comparable range of facilities. But to recognise this would be to introduce a socio-geographic parameter into the quest for the right answer . . . and that would make the unitary principle inapplicable to any of the more populous parts of the country.[65]

Maud Applies its Principles

The Maud Commission stuck pretty well to its population range. Of the fifty eight one-tier authorities only three are over the upper limit of 1,000,000 and only five under 250,000. Slightly over half of them lay in the range 250,000 to 500,000. The outstanding exceptions to the rule were, of course Selnec (South East Lancashire, North East Cheshire), Merseyside and the West Midlands. In those metropolitan authorities special arrangements were made breaking the principle of a one-tier system.

Let us take some examples of the ways in which the general principles of the main report worked out. It seems reasonable to look at three types: the sparsely populated rural area, the highly populated area where the centre is a large town and the area where there is no single large centre of population but where the population is concentrated in a number of smaller settlements.

Let us take the area of low population density first. Unit 43, Norwich and Norfolk, covers a large area of marshland. It contains three towns of considerable independent importance, Norwich, Great Yarmouth and King's Lynn and a number of not unimportant towns: for example, Beccles, Lowestoft and Thetford. It covers an area of 2,157 square miles and, in 1968, it had a population of 687,000. Clearly it is a large area but more important than its size is the distribution of its population and the features of social geography. It would have been possible to have made an acceptable out of Norwich and the surrounding countryside. This would have given a population figure of around 400,000; but it would have cut off Great Yarmouth along with the other fishing towns and given a population which was undersized by the standards of the Commission. The same difficulty would almost certainly have arisen in the case of King's Lynn which cannot really be shown to have a closer tie with any other town. In short a city region has not emerged.

How would Senior have dealt with the same area? In the first place Senior accepted neither the unitary principle nor the main Commission's population ranges as God-given. In a section on 'size and performance' he points out that, although there was an implicit assumption in the setting up of the Commission that they would recommend larger units, the evidence of their own research workers pointed in another direction.

Indeed, some of the findings of Research Study No. 3 in respect of particular types of existing local authority 'suggest the opposite of what has been the common view about the effects of an increase in the population or size of a local authority on its efficiency. The refute not only the prevalent view that economics of scale would be achieved by increasing the present size of such local authorities but also provide some evidence that diseconomies of scale operate with an increase in the population size.' Others strongly refute the notion of an optimum size.

Research Study No. 4's exhaustive analysis of twenty-seven performance indices in relation to fifteen measurable characteristics of local authorities produced only one significant finding that held good for both counties and county boroughs and that was the unexpected one that large education authorities do not exploit their potential advantage of being able to afford a higher proportion of specialist advisers.[66]

Senior's equivalent to the Commission's Unit 43 is region 22: Norwich. It has an area of 2,240 square miles and a population of 786,000 in 1968. In other words the areas chosen to illustrate the two schemes are more or less similar. Senior, of course, opts for a two-tier solution and there is a Regional council looking after police, education, some aspects of housing and so on. The district councils look after smaller areas within the total boundary. There are three of these: Norwich City and the surrounding countryside, Great Yarmouth along with other smaller fishing towns and their hinterland, and Kings Lynn and a similar stretch of countryside around that borough. Of these Norwich is by far the largest with a population of 403,000 while Great Yarmouth has 167,000 and Kings Lynn has 117,000. There are quite large disparities of size among the districts but the organising principle of attaching areas to towns which are within easy reach is maintained. Senior goes into several differences of principle in considerable detail. The overall point is that in an area of sparse population, a very large area has to be covered to take in the required number of people which is bound to lead to a long travelling distance between many points in the unit and what is supposed to be its centre. It may also lead to the area not having one centre but several.

Let us now turn to an area of medium population density, Unit 52: Reading and Berkshire. Here in an area of 879 square miles there was in 1968 a population of 794,000. Here there are many

boroughs of varying character; but Reading is the most important.
Whereas in the previous example the towns are divided by large
distances, in Berkshire the centres are easily acessible. But they all
have different characters and it is difficult to say that any of them,
with the exception of Reading, stands out as the 'capital' or should
come into this area rather than into another. For example, Slough,
at one end of the proposed unit, has more obvious ties with the
London metropolitan area than it has with Reading. Basingstoke, at
the other, might as easily go with Guildford. It is a bi-polar unit and not
an area which conveniently arranges itself around some clearly
dominant population centre.

Let us turn to the densely populated parts of the country.
In three of these the Commission made other arrangements and so
admitted that the unitary solution is not a universal solution.

In the West of Yorkshire there is a heavy concentration of
population centring around the towns of Leeds, Bradford,
Huddersfield, Halifax, Dewsbury and Wakefield. The Commission
was aware of this and considered whether to propose a
metropolitan organisation.

> We found, however, that the West Yorkshire towns differ from
> those of Merseyside, Selnec and the West Midlands for geographical
> and historical reasons. The West Yorkshire conurbation is looser
> in its physical and economic structure. It contains more open
> land . . . The independent growth and character of the West
> Yorkshire towns is illustrated by the fact only nine miles from
> Leeds with its half-million population there has grown up the
> conurbation's second city of Bradford, with nearly 300,000
> filling to some extent a parallel role and a focus for smaller
> places around it.[67]

To deal with this area the Commission proposed five independent
units: Bradford, Leeds, Halifax, Huddersfield and Mid-Yorkshire,
Units 7-11.

Senior takes the alternative approach of using one regional council
to look after the whole area (Region 4 Leeds) with eight districts:
Leeds (698,000), Pontefract (190,000), Wakefield (137,000),
Dewsbury (174,000), Huddersfield (207,000), Halifax (306,000),
Bradford (365,000) and Skipton (137,000). Such a pattern might have
been followed by the Commission had they decided to make the
government of this area metropolitan in form. Senior would argue
that, whereas the main report led to an over-rigid formula for the
authorities, with the two-tier system it was possible to recognise the
close inter-dependence of the parts of this conurbation by
establishing a regional authority and at the same time to recognise
the diversity of the parts by making provision for district councils.

Let us turn to the three metropolitan areas. These were the West Midlands, including Birmingham, Wolverhampton, Walsall, Dudley and West Bromwich, Selnec (which consisted of Manchester, Altrincham, Stockport, Bolton, Oldham, Bury, Rochdale, Warrington and Wigan), and Merseyside (consisting of Liverpool, St. Helens, Widnes, Southport and Crosby). In these areas there was a proposal for a two-tier system of local government.

Intensive study of the information relating to the Merseyside, Selnec and West Midlands conurbations and to the areas around them showed that the magnitude and complexity of these issues there require units for planning, transportation and major development whose territory and population together are too big for a unitary authority.[68]

It is interesting to compare what Senior makes of such areas with the proposals of the main body of Commissioners. For the latter the Selnec metropolitan area consists of 1,043 square miles and in 1968 it contained 3,232,000 people. Senior's equivalent is Region 10 with 1,047 square miles and 3,122,000 of a population. The Commission proposed breaking down this unit into nine districts. Senior recommends twelve. The distribution of functions between the tiers is not the same in the two schemes. In Maud, education goes to the lower-tier level, the districts: whereas Senior recommends that this is a function which only the top tier can perform. In the distribution of the social welfare services both Senior and Maud are agreed that this should be a job for the lower tier. Wheatley in Scotland gives these services to their upper tier, leaving the district authorities with even less to do than their English equivalents under the Senior scheme.

The main report treats the lower-tier authorities as much more substantial bodies than Senior allows them to be. Perhaps in this they follow the London reorganisation. In terms of the structure, Senior and Maud also differ. In the West Midlands conurbation Maud recommends seven metropolitan districts while Senior recommends twelve but for an area which is almost three times the size. Senior takes a much wider view of the regional pull of this conurbation including such towns as Shrewsbury and Worcester and their surrounding areas.

Both Maud and Senior recommend radical changes to local government. But Senior was right in his criticism of the main report when he said that they had stuck to the proposition that 'bigger meant better' even when it was clear from their own research studies, especially numbers three, four and five, that there was no correlation at all.

Any doubts about the government's intentions concerning Maud were dispelled by the publication of the White Paper, *Reform of Local*

Government in England,[69] in 1970. The major amendments which it
made to Maud were a reduction in the number of unitary authorities to
fifty-one and the addition of two new metropolitan areas in West
Yorkshire (the Leeds area) and South West Hampshire (Southampton
and Portsmouth). The idea of unitary authorities as a norm was
accepted. 'Adoption of the unitary system wherever it is practical
will make local government more efficient and more comprehensible to
the public.'[70] The government made some changes in the distribution
of functions between metropolitan authorities and the metropolitan
districts and indicated that it did not think it was appropriate that
local councils should run any services.

The road to reform was, however, not straight. In June 1970, the
Conservative Party was returned to power and with an only
half-formulated policy but one clearly opposed to unitary authorities.

Reform and the Conservatives

With the excitement of the election, local government reform inevitably
took a second place. When people began to think about it again there
was a great deal of speculation that reorganisation might never happen.
The last few years had, however, created an atmosphere in which
change of some sort was inevitable. The Whitehall machine had been
geared to it. The new Conservative government too, had come in
with the proclaimed intention of creating a more efficient system of
government in Britain. Peter Walker, the new Minister, in particular
was associated with the notion of efficient government. In October 1970
he made a statement in the House of Commons to the effect that
legislation would be considered not later than the 1972-73 session.[71]
He announced that a Ministerial committee was working on the
subject and that a White Paper was to appear soon.

It was published in February 1971.[72] The fact that a two-tier
system was recommended came as not surprise but some other aspects
of the proposals were interesting. First, many of the principles of the
Redcliffe Maud Commission had been maintained. For example, the
districts which were proposed unified town and country areas:
county boroughs were to disappear, and there were to be special
'metropolitan' arrangements for highly urbanised areas: Merseyside,
Selnec, the West Midlands, West Yorkshire, South Yorkshire and the
Tyne and Wear area (South Hampshire had been dropped, South
Yorkshire and Tyne were added). Of them the White Paper said:

> These six areas need to be treated as entities for purposes of
> planning, transportation and certain other services; at the
> same time, the districts into which they divide would be big
> enough in population and resources and even sufficiently

compact in size to be responsible for education and the personal
services as well as the more local functions.
It was recognised that there were a number of special cases and the
division of functions in these areas should be different.

The question of the distribution of functions was, of course,
important for the non-metropolitan areas too. Here the government
was more generous to the districts than had been expected. They
were to get the important housing service with the counties having only
reserve powers (for special circumstances, such as overspill). In planning
they were to have development control but the officers serving them
were to be part of a unified planning staff serving the counties
too. These latter 'upper-tier' authorities were to have the
'development of both structure and local plans', otherwise district
authorities were to be responsible for refuse collection and to share
environmental health, museums and art galleries, parks and open spaces,
playing fields and swimming baths, and coast protection with the
counties. They were to be responsible for highways, traffic and
transport, education, libraries and personal social services. Police and
fire services would also be county functions although there would
be amalgamations in several cases.

The spirit of Maud had been retained by putting the important
local functions at the upper or county level. The exceptions to this
were of course housing, and, to a lesser extent, planning. It was
argued that housing was such an important service and so closely
linked to the main planning function that it should have been given
to the counties. From the point of view of the lower, non-metropolitan,
tier it could be argued that social work was really a job for an
authority operating at a more intimate level and that, in any case, it was
so closely linked with housing that once the decision had been made to
position this function in the district, the other function should
follow it. Similarly it was argued that libraries need not be so large as
to require to be operated by the county.

Simultaneously with the White Paper there was published a
circular[73] which set out the proposed boundaries for the new
counties and metropolitan districts. The White Paper commented:

> It must be emphasised that the new counties will in no sense
> be a continuation of the existing county authorities. They will
> be entirely new authorities binding together — in most cases
> for the first time — all of the urban and rural areas within
> their boundaries. Where possible, existing county boundaries
> will be retained in order to keep the meximum existing loyalties
> and to minimise the administrative problems.[74]

Map 1 indicates the extent to which most county authorities were left
intact. As far as this part of the reorganisation was concerned it seems

that the government was rather timid. It abandoned altogether the idea
that was canvassed during the work of the commission that the areas
of authorities should be founded upon the social geography of the
country rather than the traditional boundaries. Maud followed this
principle less than did Senior's minority report but, in the maps
accompanying the White Paper, there was an even clearer move away
from it. County boundaries were widely retained. Nowhere was this
'county bias' to be seen more clearly than in the way in which
metropolitan areas were treated. The lines were drawn more tightly
around these large urbanised areas than Maud had recommended.
Once again the demands of urban centres seem to have been
disregarded so that the counties could retain their territories.

In an article in the *Municipal Journal*,[75] Derek Senior analysed the
boundary proposals and demonstrated the haphazard nature of the
town and country mixture for the proposed areas. Where the original
idea had been that the entire hinterland of an urban area should be
brought in, Senior showed that in many cases only part of this
hinterland was attached to the urban service centre. In Plymouth,
Brighton, Peterborough, Milton Keynes, Luton, Stoke and Teeside,
for example, he showed that only about half of the hinterland had
been taken in. When the Bill was published in November 1971 this
process of restricting the urban areas had gone even further. Again
it was particularly evident in the metropolitan areas. For example,
Ellesmere Port was taken out of Merseyside and Harrogate from West
Yorkshire. Senior argued very cogently that such an approach showed
that this was a 'political deal' sort of approach rather than one that
recognised new patterns of living. In particular, by drawing the
boundaries so tightly around the metropolitan areas the new
government ignored the town and country war which had been
going on at least since the beginning of the century.

In other ways the government showed its caution. This was going
to be an extremely contentious bill and, in order to get over the
problem of a cluttered Parliamentary time-table, the
Minister responsible, Graham Page, had a series of face-to-face
discussions all around the country with local government interests.
In this way a great deal of Parliamentary time was saved but the
procedure also meant that the views of the local authorities had much
more effect on the final drawing of boundaries than would have been
the case if the Maud pattern had been followed by a Labour
government. Peter Walker's regional conferences with Conservative
local government personnel set the pattern for his later dealing
with local authorities. When the Bill was published there was some
complaint from local authorities but it was by no means a flood.

This acceptance of local authority pressure was exemplified in other

differences between the Bill and the White Paper. More services were
placed at district level. The main change here was in planning. For
practical purposes the idea of a unified planning staff was abandoned
and each type of authority was allowed to have its own. Districts were
given the right to frame their own 'local plans' within the structure
plan formulated by the county in consultation with the districts.
Building control was also given to the districts along with the
operation of clean air programmes and all environmental health
responsibilities. At a rather less important level districts were given
responsibility for unclassified urban roads and they became the
rating authority along with the borough in metropolitan areas.

Many people had hoped that the Bill would extend the
system of parish councils to other areas. This was not done specifically.
Section 27 of the Bill directed that there should be a community
council for areas which already had parish councils. For boroughs or
urban districts which were 'free standing' and had been swallowed up
in a new district there could be community councils if the
Secretary of State deemed fit. For other areas the Bill was silent.
In the passage of the Bill through Parliament there were few major
changes. One of the most striking was that the Isle of Wight was given
separate island status during consideration by the Lords. This was the
result of a long period of publicity managed by a public relations
firm.[76] Many of the aspects of this were reminiscent of the earlier
activities of Rutland. Other changes were, perhaps, more important.

There was a great deal of discussion on urban parishes or communities.
At the beginning Graham Page, for the government, was not
encouraging but, on pressure from Labour and Conservative members,
the situation changed. He announced, for example,[77] that the district
councils which were to review parish arrangements could do so in
both urban and rural areas. The powers of parish councils were
somewhat enlarged as compared with those before the Act. All
parishes were to have powers which were previously adoptive and they
were also to have powers to provide public lavatories and off-street
car parking, to encourage public entertainment, arts and crafts,
tourism and conferences. They were also given the right to see all
planning applications which affected their area.

Perhaps the function which caused most controversy was planning.
The idea of a unified planning staff was abandoned and in this way it
was made more certain that districts would have control over their
own planning. Because this increased the number of planning
authorities from 141 to 401 the government agreed that, in the event
of a dispute between county and district planning they would be
incluned to view the county plan more sympathetically.[78]

Appendix 1 shows the distribution of functions between the types

of authorities as they stood at the end of Parliamentary proceedings.
Map 1 shows the final assignment of boundaries. During the
Committee stage the government showed itself to be flexible about
boundaries and there was a great deal of discussion about them.
In this context, the work of the Local Government Boundary
Commission should be mentioned. This body was set up by the Act
but in fact started to operate under the chairmanship of
Sir Edmund Compton before the legislation was passed. It is a
permanent body with the duty of reviewing boundaries every ten to
fifteen years. Its first review of district boundaries was completed
in five months. As a general guideline it was agreed that no district
should have less than 40,000 inhabitants except in exceptional cases.
In their first report all the proposed districts were over this minimum.
In general, the report stuck closely to existing boundaries largely, it
appeared, because it depended upon proposals from existing
county authorities. The areas which suffered most were ex-county
boroughs, which were denied extra territory. Out of forty-two claims
for this kind of extension only thirteen were successful.

The Nature of the Act

The Act represented a great change from the previous situation.
There was a great deal of consolidation and amalgamation of local
authorities; but it was a less radical solution than Maud's. It stuck
to existing boundaries rather than conceding to the facts of
social geography. Senior would, of course, have claimed that even
Maud was not radical enough in this regard. The two-tier approach
was concocted to appeal to the maximum number of
sympathetic local government interests. Indeed, in its whole
approach to reform, this government seemed much more inclined
to consult and compromise than had its predecessor. Labour, of
course, was not involved in bringing in a Bill with all its attendant
negotiation and horse-trading. Nevertheless, its acceptance of Maud in
the teeth of quite strenuous local government reaction suggests that
Labour was prepared to take a strong centralising line. The Conservatives
went through many phases of consultation. They showed themselves
sensitive to local claims not only on the question of boundaries
where, on the whole, they interpreted the Act in terms of the county
interest, but also on other questions where there were strong local
government points of view. They were, for example, slow to abandon
the office of alderman. This did not come until the publication of the
Bill itself and even then aldermen were kept for the City of London
against opposition from some Conservative MPs.

It was in line with this that, when the Secretary of State for the

Environment introduced the Bill in the second reading, he paid tribute to local government and pointed out that over 400 central controls were to be lifted. The reform would be a liberating measure for local government. It is necessary to put such a claim in perspective. It is true that many of the mechanical restraints were lifted. More flexibility was introduced, for example, in the question of the Committees which local authorities had to appoint. They were no longer required to appoint Health, Finance, Allotments, Diseases of Animals and Youth Employment Committees. On the other hand, the vital question of finance was untouched.

When Maud was set up the Prime Minister made it clear that finance was not in its remit. This was the traditional pattern since the question of the revenue of local government was also considered and dealt with by interdepartmental consultations rather than by an independent advisory body. In these interdepartmental negotiations the Treasury was clearly going to be very important.

In the Green Paper which was published in July 1971[79] the pros and cons of various systems were set out. On balance it was agreed that the existing rating system whould be improved (e.g. by the superrating of non-domestic properties or the idea that assessment might be on capital rather than on renting values) rather than that new systems like a local income tax should be introduced. In so far as the Bill dealt with finance at all it simply retained the rating system with all its known problems. The one notable change was that the district auditor was no longer necessary. Districts could offer an approved auditor. Similarly, the district auditor could not now surcharge if he believed that circumstances dictated this. Instead he had to go to the courts with any such problems.

There are certainly many observers who would argue that such an arrangement made nonsense of the idea that the legislation in any sense freed local government from central control. Rates as a form of revenue are too inflexible to meet the financial demands of local services. The system ensures central control because local authorities cannot finance themselves without supplementation from central government. When it is considered that the reduction of the number of local authorities made central control easier, it can be claimed that local government reform was regarded in Whitehall as a means of ensuring better co-ordination and management. An equivalent development on the central government side was the consolidation of many of the supervisory functions of central government over local authorities. This was achieved by the establishment of the Department of the Environment in the autumn of 1970, which brought together the powers over planning, housing, the regions and transport. Furthermore, during the time that the Local Government

Bill was being debated, powers were being stripped from the new councils. A Report[80] argued that water had to be regionally managed and that the boundaries of these regions could not be the same as county boundaries since they would have to follow the lines of watersheds and water catchment areas. (In the *Municipal Journal* of 14 January 1972, Derek Senior argued that there was little difficulty in aligning these catchment areas with provincial boundaries.)

Similarly, in February 1972, a White Paper appeared announced the long-awaited plans for the future of the Health Service.[81] Far from hospitals being given back to local authorities most of the remaining local authority health functions were to be taken away from them and to be administered by non-elected regional and area authorities. Medical Officers of Health were to disappear. It became difficult to think of a local government system revived and strengthened by the new measures. Indeed, at a time when corporate management and the integrated approach to problems were both vogue terms, the government had made this impossible by a return to nineteenth-century 'ad hocery'. Of the other fashionable ideas of 'accountability' and 'participation' there appeared to be very little left.

There was never any discussion of the possibility of electoral reform in local government. This is a topic which has cropped up continuously in British politics. It has never been favourably regarded by the major parties. Nor was any of the major figures in local government in favour of it. They might have looked at the experience of other countries — indeed they might have looked at the experience of Northern Ireland where, in 1920, two elections were fought at the local government level in January and June of that year on a single transferable vote system. This system was set up by the Local Government (Ireland) Bill, 1919 and the experience of 1920 is fully discussed in *Regional Representation in Urban Electors in Ulster*[82] and in *Local Government Elections in Northern Ireland.*[83]

NOTES

1. *Problems of Social Policy*, HMSO and Longmans, London, p.17. See also Chapter 11 for a discussion of the problem.
2. Ibid., p.203.
3. *Public Service*, December 1940.
4. See above (chapter on Planning).
5. House of Commons Debates, vol. 402, col. 157?.
6. Cmnd. 6579/45.
7. House of Commons Debates, vol. 410, col 1961.

8. 'Members of the Commission discovered in their investigation that, every time they considered boundaries, functions came up all over the country . . . After some discussion I agreed that they could go outside the terms of reference and make a report which would call attention to the necessity of an alteration of functions and boundaries and make some adumbrations on the reform of local government.' Mr. Bevan in a speech winding up the Second Reading of the Local Government Boundary Commission (Dissolution) Bill, House of Commons Debates, vol. 469, cols. 515-6.

9. House of Commons Debates, 1947-48, col. 86.

10. Ibid., para. 39.

11. Ibid., para. 1.

12. House of Commons Paper 1948-49, no. 150, para. 4.

13. 30 November 1946.

14. Vol. 154, 17 April 1948, p. 622.

15. House of Commons Debates, vol. 466, col. 758.

16. House of Commons Debates, vol. 469, col. 410.

17. *First Report of the Local Government Manpower Committee*, Cmnd. 7870/1960, para. 1.

18. In a written reply, House of Commons Debates, vol. 588, cols. 170-71.

19. Cmnd. 9831/56.

20. *Functions of County Councils and County District Councils*, Cmnd. 161/57, and *Local Government Finance*, Cmnd. 209/57.

21. House of Commons Debates, vol. 579, cols. 901-1020, and 1085-1199.

22. Ibid., col. 924.

23. Cmnd. 209, para. 3.

24. *Local Government Commission Regulations*, 21 November 1958.

25. 'The Local Government Commission and County Boroughs Extensions', *Public Administration*, vol. 41, 1963, pp. 173-87.

26. *Report and Proposals for the East Midlands General Review Area*, HMSO, London, 1961, p.8.

27. Ibid., p. 18.

28. Jones, p. 175.

29. Jones, p. 175.

30. 19 July 1960.

31. *Royal Commission on Local Government in Greater London*, Cmnd. 1164, HMSO, London, 1960.

32. See Frank Smallwood, *Greater London, The Politics of Metropolitan Reform*, Merrill, New York, 1965.

33. Ibid., p. 1.

34. Ibid., p. 99.

35. 'County Borough Expansion. The Local Government Commission's Views', *Public Administration*, vol. 42, 1964, p. 277.

36. HMSO, London, 1963.

37. *Traffic in Towns* (Shortened Version), Penguin, London, 1964, p. 15.

38. 24 April 1965.
39. 14 September 1965.
40. Reprinted as 'The Future of Local Government', *Public Administration,* vol. 40, 1962, p. 375-86.
41. Cmnd. 1728/62, *Management of Local Government,* HMSO (Ministry of Housing and Local Government), London, 1967.
42. *Staffing of Local Government,* HMSO (Ministry of Housing and Local Government), London, 1964.
43. *Why Local Democracy?* Fabian Tract 361, Fabian Society, London, 1965.
44. *New Life for Local Government,* Conservative Political Centre, London, 1965.
45. Cmnd. 5460/73.
46. House of Commons Debates, vol. 724, col. 640.
47. *Local Government in England and Wales,* Hutchinsons University Library, London, 2nd ed., 1953.
48. Longmans, London, 1966.
49. *Royal Commission on Local Government in England. Written evidence of the Ministry of Housing and Local Government,* paras. 40-41.
50. *Royal Commission on Local Government in England, Evidence of H.M. Treasury,* para. 8.
51. Cmnd. 3333/67.
52. Cmnd. 4040/69.
53. Cmnd. 5050-1/69.
54. *Royal Commission on Local Government in Scotland,* Cmnd. 4150/69, HMSO, Edinburgh.
55. Maud, para. 299.
56. Maud, para. 371.
57. Maud, para. 382.
58. Maud, para. 383.
59. Senior, para. 4.
60. Senior, para. 5.
61. Senior, para. 123.
62. Senior, para. 18.
63. Senior, para. 33.
64. Senior, para. 559.
65. Senior, para. 19.
66. Senior, para. 265-6.
67. Maud, Annex 1, p. 193.
68. Maud, para. 289.
69. Cmnd. 4276/70.
70. Ibid., para. 18.
71. House of Commons Debates, vol. 805, col. 331.
72. *Local Government in England,* Cmnd. 4584/71, HMSO, London
73. Circular 8/71.
74. Cmnd. 4584, para. 29.
75. 26 March 1971.
76. Walbrooks Ltd.

77.   1 February 1972. Standing Committee D, cols. 1170-79.
78.   24 February 1972. Standing Committee D, cols. 1902-3.
79   *The Future Shape of Local Government Finance,* Cmnd. 4741,
        HMSO, London, 1971.
80.   *The Future Management of Water in England and Wales,*
        Central Advisory Water Committee, HMSO, London, 1971.
81.   *National Health Services Reorganisation:* England,
        Cmnd. 5055/1972, HMSO, London.
82.   Ulster Committee of the Proportional Representation Society
        of Ireland, 1920. Reprinted by The Electoral Reform Society,
        London, 1972.
83.   Electoral Reform Society, London. Both this and the former
        publication are available from the Society at 6 Chancel Street,
        Southwark, London, SE1 0UX.

3 THE LOCAL GOVERNMENT ASSOCIATIONS AND REFORM

We now have a picture of how events developed. What part was played by the local government associations? Were they the major forces resisting reform? It is necessary to find out who they were and what they represented.

The Nature of the Associations

The Association of Municipal Corporations was born in 1873. Acting on behalf of Sheffield Corporation, Mr. Leemans introduced a Bill to enable municipal corporations to promote Acts of Parliament by means of funds raised from general rates. The point of this Bill, which was was the basis of the *Burgh Funds Act* of 1872, was to enable corporations to buy gas and water companies. It was defeated by an amendment which gave the powers requested only if the resulting companies would not be in competition with other companies. This caused great consternation. The Parliamentary Committee of the Borough of Nottingham was authorised by its council to take any action for 'promoting the unity of action of municipal corporations for maintaining their privileges and resisting encroachment on their prerogatives.' The movement for a strong association got off the ground when the Town Clerks of Liverpool and Manchester were instructed by their councils to arrange a meeting in London. This was attended by representatives of sixty corporations including the City of London and fifty-eight MPs of both main parties. It had two outcomes. A deputation was sent to the Home Secretary and the President of the Local Government Board. Secondly, an Association of Municipal Corporations was set up. Thus, the AMC was the first of the local government associations and was founded specifically to look after the privileges of the municipal corporations, the major units of local government at that time. Rule 2(1) stated:

> The objectives of the Association are, by complete organisation, more effectively to watch over and protect the interests, rights and privileges of municipal corporations as they may be affected by private and public bill legislation of general application to brooughs and in other subjects to take action in relation to other subjects in which municipal corporations may be interested.

There is not much doubt that this action had party political overtones. In a letter concerning the original Bill, A.J. Mundella (one of the MPs for Sheffield) wrote

> The opposition of the Tories and the (water) companies is very
> bitter. The Tories hate the boroughs and Municipal Corporations.
> The former return Radical MPs the latter petition for Ballot
> and other obnoxious bills and are always wanting sewage farms
> and interfering with fishing by polluting streams. The number
> of Lords who have a grudge against and litigation pending with
> boroughs is surprising.[1]

While the AMC was founded to protect members against encroachment
of their rights, the County Council Association was set up to reinforce
and extend the increase in powers given under the Local Government
Act of 1888. This second association was not without its ancestors.
A Society of Clerks of the Peace of Counties was set up in 1810 to
remedy the irksomeness of the duties imposed upon them by the
government in 1780. By 188, it had become so well established as an
advisory body that, when the Local Government Bill was drafted, this
draft was sent to them for comment. Over 100 amendments which they
suggested were incorporated. It was on the initiative of this body that
the CCA was set up. At a meeting of the Society on 13 June 1889, it
was resolved that:

> Clerks of the Peace be recommended to bring before their
> respective Councils a resolution to the effect that it is
> desirable to establish an Association of County Councils
> similar to the Association of Municipal Corporations.

The degree to which the CCA was modelled on the AMC is to be seen
by comparing its major object with the stated object of the AMC which
has already been quoted:

> By complete organisation more effectively to watch over and
> protect the interests, rights and privileges of the County
> Councils as representatives of the county ratepayers as they may
> be affected by legislation, public or private, of general
> application to the counties.

Of the two associations, the CCA had least in the way of internal
problems. The AMC was split by the fact that it contained at least
two major types of authority whose interests did occasionally clash:
the county boroughs and the non-county boroughs. Of these the
non-county boroughs were by far the largest number with 310
authorities in membership, about three-quarters of the total
membership. The divided nature of the organisation can be seen if
one looks at its composition. Its council consisted of sixty-eight
county boroughs(the five largest and sixty-three of the others),
sixty eight non-county boroughs (including five with a population
under 10,000), seventeen metropolitan boroughs, one borough from
Northern Ireland and the City of London. Parity of representation

on the Council of the county and non-county boroughs was
introduced in 1890 while the arrangements to guarantee the
representation of the small boroughs was only brought in in 1944.
One of the main difficulties was over attitudes to reorganisation. In
fact, separate organisations to represent the interests of the two
major types were set up; a County Boroughs Association and a
Non-County Boroughs Committee of the AMC.

Although for the record there were only two types of borough
in the AMC, using other, more political criteria we could distinguish
six. First there were the very large county boroughs like Manchester
and Birmingham which were so big they could contemplate a
metropolitan two-tier solution to their problems. Below them were the
expanding county boroughs whose need was for housing land but
whose ideal form of government was still the one-tier system.
Thirdly, amongst the county boroughs, there were the small and
weak who feared that any reform would mean their disappearance.
Among the non-county boroughs, too, three types emerge: the very
large ones who, from their size, could hope for promotion to
autonomous status; medium-sized non-county boroughs who
worked for more powers within a two-tier status and, finally, the
very smallest boroughs who wanted no change at all since reform
would kill them. All these different interests lived uneasily together
within the AMC.

During the Second World War, the Secretary of the AMC was
Sir Harry Pritchard. The office of Parliamentary Agent to the
Association had been in this family for many years and when Sir Harry
ceased to be Secretary, he carried on the other office for some time.
Sir Harold Banwell, who succeeded him, had been Town Clerk of
Lincoln and County Clerk of Lincolnshire (parts of Kesteven). He was
a man of great energy, and even after he retired in 1962, took an
active part in the life of local government. The next Secretary,
J.C. Shawfield, was Town Clerk of Blackpool and came into his post
with some new and radical ideas.

The first Secretary of the CCA to concern us was Sir Sidney Johnson,
who steered the Association through the war years 1939-45. From his
correspondence, he appears to have viewed county government rather
in the fashion of the old gentry. He brusquely dismissed any attempts
from groups other than the main associations to put forward their
views on reogrnisation. Thus, for example, the National Association of
Local Government Officers' plan and that of the County Engineers
Association were treated as impertinences. His successor, W. Dacey,
was forced into a less exclusive position by the pressure of events. It
was he who formed an allegiance between his own association and
that of the "Urbans" and the "Rurals" and eventually the National

Association of Parish Councils, in favour of a two-tier solution to the problem of reform. By dint of years of negotiations, he finally led them to a scheme which was mutually acceptable. If we look at the 1958 Local Government Act, it is surprising how near it is to his original ideas. In 1964 he was killed in a motor accident and A.C. Hetherington, then County Clerk of Cheshire, took his place.

The Rural District Councils and the Urban District Councils both had their own associations. They were not so important as those mentioned above but they did organise the interests of their members. Perhaps the most interesting difference between them was that the RDCA tended to be more of an elected members' organisation where the "urbans" was more of an officer-dominated body. The National Association of Parish Councils looked after the interests of the parishes.

The history of attempted reform since 1945 is the story of a struggle between the AMC on the one side and an alliance of CCA, UDCA, and RDCA on the other side. It is this conflict between the larger towns and the rest which will be a main concern in this chapter.

Stengths and Weaknesses of the Associations

A number of general themes will emerge in the course of this chapter. They are listed briefly.

First the associations were continually squabbling over the course which reform should take. There were many topics on which they could co-operate, such as local government services and the increase of central grant to authorities. The subject of reform did not, however, lend itself to an alliance because each considered its best interests to be in some sense in conflict with one or other of the rest. Each one initially saw its duty as the defence of all of its members, however small and inefficient. This is, after all, what a good protective organisation should do but it can also be argued that compromise is a good strategy. All the associations can be accused of unwillingness to compromise. Even when it is necessary for the survival of local government as a whole that they should make common cause, they did not do so.

There is a subsidiary point here. Within each organisation there were "hard-liners" who took a different position from that of the leadership. In the AMC the position was somewhat more difficult in that it contained both county and non-county boroughs. Thus in schemes for reform where one type of authority would gain, the other was opposed. This inevitably held up co-operation because the AMC could reach no truly agreed policy of its own. Where non-county boroughs would have been quite happy to do a deal with the County Councils Associations, they were held up by the opposition of their fellow members who were county boroughs.

The second theme in the debate between the associations concerned the merits of a one- or two-tier system. There was of course discussion about how functions should be split between two tiers. Apart from this, however, was the question of whether there should be any split at all. This debate was to continue right down to the report of the Redcliffe Maud Commission and beyond it. The county boroughs were for a one-tier system and the rest were for two tiers.

Another theme is that, although the rank and file might not agree that reform was necessary and although all within the associations might have different pictures of the future they preferred, there was always an understanding of the need for reform among the *leaders.* Thus we have the very long-drawn-out negotiations in the 1940s and 1950s. As we get nearer to the present day, the leadership becomes more committed to reform and even abandons the cause of its members who by contemporary values did not come up to standards of size or quality of provision.

Finally, in defence of their interests, the spokesmen of various types of local government unit were able to appeal to certain values which were given a high position in British life, democracy, community and representation.

The vast majority of people involved in local government wanted little change in the system at least as far as it concerned them. There was a fairly widespread agreement that some reform was necessary but, if one looks at the plans for reform which were put forward by the local government associations, each association suggested a solution which might involve an upheaval for the other classes of local authority but little if any for its own members. Thus, as will be seen, the AMC had a plan which involved the complete dismantling of the county system. The CCA similarly had a scheme which would have demoted to county district level all but the large county boroughs. Most people in local government argued that, at least as far as their own area was concerned, nothing much was wrong with local government. Successive Ministers took no steps toward reform because of lack of co-operation from the associations.

In order to see why it was that the associations were able to hold up reform we must turn to the second point. Why were these groups able to put up such effective resistance when their own position was attacked? In the literature on pressure groups there are many discussions of the resources which can strengthen the arguments each interest puts forward. Finer[2], for example, distinguished between the "interest" and the "cause group". In these terms it is very clear that the local government associations are a protective group with all the inherent strengths which that implies. They are not dependent upon the altruistic feelings of their members but upon the fact that they represent the interest of the members themselves. They are not concerned with plans for some nebulous future but rather with the position of some group which is already part of the pattern of things as they are. We may spell out some of the implications of this position.

It makes sense to ask of any group, whom it is representing and to what extent it speaks for all of the "interest". In the case of protective groups such as the local government associations, the "interest" of the "public" is usually quite clearly defined. Its re representatives are in a strong position if they are known to speak for a membership which is united. With only a few exceptions, all local authorities were members of their associations and the leaders could usually claim to speak for all their members. To strengthen their position even further, for a great deal of the time the associations were agreed on the line that they would take to persuade or advise the Minister. Thus they were taken to represent the local government interest in the country against any contrary view which might be taken up by, for example, the Ministry.

In this position as the spokesmen of local government they were also recognised as "experts". Finer and indeed all the writers on pressure groups have pointed out the importance of this role. They are the people who have knowledge indispensable to central government. It is not just that they have information about how their members felt, although this is an important political resource. They also have i information about how things are actually done. In Britain, central government has laid down certain standards of performance, has inspected the local authorities and has granted much of the money. But it has been local government which has run the services. The local government associations, therefore, could speak with expert knowledge about many fields and this expertise was invaluable in any national decision-taking. They had to be listened to.

Thirdly, pressure groups tend to have power in proportion to the number of times they have previously been consulted and have been acceptable in this role to those whom they want to influence. There had been a long tradition of consultation with local government associations. It was, therefore, unthinkable that reform should be planned without bringing in these bodies. Moreover, the associations knew where to go when they wanted to apply pressure. The AMC has as Vice-Presidents a group of MPs who could be counted upon to put the relevant point of view in Parliamentary debates. All the associations were in constant touch with the departments concerned with local government and knew who to approach on any topic. If the topic were important enough the associations could be sure of an interview with the Permanent

Secretary or even the Minister. Finally, local government associations had access to important points in the national decision-making structure because senior members of the national party organisations were often councillors. In rural areas this was not so important. Elsewhere, however, councillors were well represented in the hierarchy of the local Conservative, Labour and Liberal party organisations. Whenever there seemed a real possibility of change threatening county government, considerable pressure was exerted through the Conservative Party to ensure that this did not take place. In short, national organisations had to take into account the feelings of local party leaders.

A more complex resource of the associations in respect to central government was the constitutional position of local government. In law, of course, there is no doubt that local authorities are creatures of Parliament. They can be altered or removed in the normal course of law-making. On the other hand local government has an ambiguous constitutional status. It is the agent of central government and subject to constitutional change by that power but, at the same time, it is elected by the citizens, it is responsible to them and it makes policy on their behalf. It is not surprising, therefore, that many councillors and others concerned with local government speak and act as if their legislature had the same validity as the legislature of central government. Granted that it covers only a small part of the whole territory for which Parliament is responsible, but within that territory it might seem to have equivalent status. By any objective test this point of view is insupportable but it is an insight into the attitudes taken by local government spokesmen. On all sides, there is a tendency to argue that, just as Parliament could be changed only by herself so also local government must have the last word in her own transformation.

Finally, local government takes much of its strength from its symbolic position as the guardian of certain values in British society. Here it is only necessary to point out that the associations always used this fact as a particularly important part of their argument. Thus we shall see them appealing to the value of democratic participation when defending the smallness of some of their members. Similarly, when it was suggested that certain services should be taken away from local control, local government is cited as a counter-weight to the overwhelming power of Whitehall. In other words, local government is given the role, much loved by the British, of underdog in the perpetual struggle of the little man against central government bureaucracy.

There is, of course, another side to this story. Modernisation of the structure took place and the oppostion of the vested interests was either over-ridden or modified. Thus when the Maud Commission reported and the Labour government virtually accepted its recommendations, it appeared that the associations would have to accept the situation. The pressure groups which had appeared able to obstruct moves to local government reform, were, in the short run, defeated. How was it that they lost their strength?

First of all the values which the existing system symbolised came to be less important. Other than for the people involved in local government and for a very small section of the general population, the importance of one's own locality is declining in modern society. Similarly, most citizens are probably more interested in the right of their own local authority to run it. Most citizens know less about local government than they do about central government. Thus the symbolic importance of local government has been weakened. As for the argument that local government was, with Parliament, a fundamental part of the British Constitution, the low turn-out at most local government elections seemed to argue that, if political institutions are finally legitimated by public opinion, something was far wrong with local government. In the long run this was bound to weaken the position of the associations. Closely linked to this point is the fact that, in arguing for or against certain schemes for reform, the associations were in danger of going beyond the sphere where their own counsel was acceptable among those whom they sought to influence. Even the most highly respected of pressure groups can step beyond the area in which it is accepted that they have a legitimate point of view. Many politicians felt that, though the associations might be experts in the local government services, when it came to decisions about reform of local government, that was a matter for central government. Only in Parliament was there authority for this decision.

Even in the field of services, the associations' position was weakened. It had become a commonplace that larger areas were needed. Nowhere was this clearer than in planning and yet an acceptance of this argument by the associations would have meant that many of their smaller members would have been abandoned. As the need for wider service areas became more marked, services were effectively taken away from the local authorities. *Ad hoc* authorities were set up for police and for water supply. The old local government units could not meet the new demands. Thus a strong case could be made out for their reorganisation.

Perhaps the most dangerous situation for a pressure group is when a split in its membership develops. To some extent, splits among the local government associations arose from the changing circumstances of local government and the need for wider areas. But, for the most part, the associations were weakened because of the built-in divisions of local government. The AMC and the CCA could not present a united front because their members represented different interests in terms of territory and rateable values. They put up schemes of reform which were quite contradictory. Even more seriously, the AMC was split within itself.

Finally, local government was not the only thing which was changing. Proposals for its reform have to be seen in the context of other changes in British society. There was an atmosphere which was favourable to the arguments for the reform of local government.[3]

1942-45

How does the history of associations over the post-war years bear out these generalisations?

In 1942 the associations were asked to discuss reform with Jowitt.[4] It was under these circumstances that each made its plans. The AMC was the first to produce a document.

In this, it argued, regional administration was suitable for wartime but not for peace. Secondly, it was accepted that the numbers of local authorities would have to be reduced since some were too small to be efficient and, in addition, there would be an advantage in reducing the numbers of classes of local authorities. What the AMC meant by this was that, wherever possible, a one-tier system on the model of the all-purpose county borough should eb set up. The two- or three-tier system, as it existed in many rural areas with the layers of county council, the county districts council and parish council, led to delay, friction and inefficiency as well as being less democratic than the county borough system. Thus the country as to be covered by a series of all-purpose authorities but there was to be no minimum population set for them. There was great vagueness about how the scheme was to be carried out in practice.

It is possible to guess how this proposal came about. We have seen that the AMC consisted of several different interests. The most prominent one was undoubtedly that of the county broughs; the single-tier, all-purpose authorities. It is hardly surprising that they should suggest that they were the epitome of all that was good in the system. In addition there were many large non-county boroughs who saw themselves as candidates for county borough status. They too would be happy to press this point of view. This second group had a somewhat indefinite membership depending on the criteria (largely population sizes) which they perceived as freeing them from the thraldom of the county. The group, therefore, overlapped with the vast majority of non-county boroughs who had no hope of ever becoming independent.

These latter were bound to the two-tier system. To include those
and keep them happy, no minimum population was mentioned. The
statement concluded that there were some situations in which the
two-tier system was better. In conurbations, in cases of small ancient
towns with charters (something with a population of around
10,000 having a charter that went back over a hundred years was
envisaged) and finally in large rural areas, the one-tier system might
not be practicable. Six criteria were suggested to test whether or not
an area was suitable. First, the area should be capable of efficiently
administering the local government services. Secondly, that
administration should also be economic. Thirdly, its financial resources
should be sufficient. Fourthly, it should be possible to reach a required
level of specialisation in all the services which the authority ran.
Fifthly, it should be possible to get good councillors and finally, the
local authority should be manageable enough to be influenced by
public opinion.

These proposals embodied many important points. Most important
of all, the division between town and country was faced and a
solution proposed. The new, all-purpose authorities were to include
rural as well as urban parts and in many areas the small country town
would be amalgamated with its hinterland which it had strong
economic and social connections. These suggestions made a great
deal of sense and it is only when viewed in political terms that one
doubts their practicality. Would the other types of local authority even
agree to this solution?

Soon, the UDCA and the RDCA contributed memoranda to the
Cabinet Committee. Both of these rejected the idea of a one-tier
system and pressed for the continuation of the county reviews which
had been begun under the Local Government Act of 1929. Both reports
pointed to the important place which their respective local
authorities played in the system.

Meanwhile the "wait and see" policy of the CCA was hard
pressed. Finally, in July 1942, the Executive Council passed a
resolution

> that in consequence of developments in other quarters (the
> memoranda of the other associations) it has become necessary for
> the association to take action in the interest of county council
> administration . . . a special committee should be set up to
> prepare a memorandum.

Thus, last of all the associations, the CCA agreed to put forward
proposals. This delaying tactic is understandable. This type of
authority had the most to lose by any re-organisation along the lines
of past developments. The over-flowing population of the towns
pointed to county borough extensions as the easiest course of

reform for the government. There were some non-county boroughs whose size, especially with the addition of suburbs technically outside the authority, made them obvious candidates for county borough status. All this threatened county status and finance. It is not surprising that the association had decided to wait. The initiative of the other bodies together with the centralisation of many local services conspired to force the CCA's hand.

In the first draft of its memorandum to the Paymaster General, the Association conceded that 100,000 was the minimum for a county. At that time this would have involved the loss of fourteen counties but the authors of the draft maintained that this need not mean the loss of historical associations or local interest. Seventy-five thousand should be the minimum population for a county borough which would then have entailed the loss of about twenty-three of these authorities. The draft rejected both the ideas of regionalism and of the one-tier authority as the norm for the whole country. It recommended that the distinction between urban and rural districts should be dropped and the single title of county district be substituted with similar powers for urban and rural areas. Their minimum size should be 10,000. On the question of functions, there were strong moves, early in the discussions, for extensions to the powers of the counties. In the end, the draft recommended that education, mental health and diseases of animals should be county and county borough functions.

As far as the smaller counties and the lower-tier authorities were concerned, this was rather fierce. When it came to be discussed by the Association in December 1942 it was attacked from several sides and indeed many of the leaders of the Association felt that it had gone too far. Small counties like Rutland and Holland objected to the minimum population set for counties and as a result of a combined attack by the seven smallest counties this section was modified, so that counties which were below this figure would be reviewed 'with a view to enquiring into the circumstances of these counties and as to their capacity to carry out their functions economically and efficiently.'

The effect of this memorandum was to cool down the relations between the CCA and the district council associations. The Secretary of the RDCA issued a letter to all clerks of Rural District Councils asking them to call together meetings to denounce the CCA proposals which he saw as destroying the 'rurals'. The Secretary of the UDCA warned that they were unacceptable.

The situation at the end of 1942 was, then, that each association had prepared a memorandum in which they sought to protect or to further the interest of their members. The proposals of the two smaller organisations were the least adventurous. During the war there

was a great deal of thinking about larger units and obviously the
lower-tier authorities were in a precarious position. Many of their
functions were taken from them and they were to lose still more
both to central government and to the counties. The proposals of the
CCA were also to a large extent in the nature of a 'holding operation'.
It envisaged no change in the basic structure of local government and
would have retained many of the structural elements which were at the
root of the problem. To a layman, the AMC solution whereby the
town-country friction was lessened through the inclusion of both
in one authority, seems more far-sighted. Unhappily, this most
radical of all the solutions was both vague and threatening to all
other types of authority and to a large section of the membership
of the AMC as well. To put forward this suggestion was to gamble on
the tenor of the political situation. If the politicians were in the mood
for a big change then it might be a practical possibility. It transpired
that they were not and the Association virtually excluded itself
from negotiations in subsequent years as a result of the stand that
it had taken.

Thus, as early as 1942 the debate on the merits of a one-tier
and two-tier system had begun. This was to continue until the
discussion on Maud. The protagonists were not to change. For the one-
tier system there was the AMC and for the two-tier, the rest. Among
the various proposals which were to be made in the future by the
other bodies, these associations tended to favour those which had the
number of tiers they favoured.

It was in line with a desire for a radical reform that in
January 1943 the AMC called for a Royal Commission to review the
whole question of local government. Given their suggestions for a
largely one-tier system, this was probably the only way to give
their proposals standing. Several counties also pressed the CCA to ask
for a Royal Commission but at this point they were not met with any
enthusiasm. The Secretary felt that it would take too long. Very soon,
however, many people active in county government became aware
that local government as a whole was being threatened. It was
rumoured that the government had plans to take away many services
from both counties and county broooughs. It was also suggested that the
government might decide that the disagreements between the local
authorities were too great and that it would simply have to impose
a solution without consulation. Thus the CCA decided to move. At the
meetings of the Executive Council in February 1943 it resolved:

> that the Executive Council could support the appointment by
> the government of a small committee, preferably with a high
> judicial authority as chairman to consider, in the light of
> memoranda submitted by the Association and such other

information as is available, the reform of local government.
In April, the CCA Executive Council resolved, on the receipt of an
invitation by the AMC that, in default of the government setting up a
committee to consider local government, the CCA would
with the other associations. This was a big step forward. Previously
there had been no consulation on this subject other than some
informal contact with the county district associations on the question
of delegation. It is important that the initial contact had been between
the counties and the county districts. In spite of the friction which
arose over delegation of powers, they were natural allies in the
fight against the inroads of the towns. Relations were always to be
closer among them on the subject of reorganisation than was the case
between the CCA and the AMC. When it was rumoured that the
Labour Party had gone over to the one-tier model of the AMC the
Secretary of the UDCA immediately contacted the CCA
representative suggesting that the should work together. The pattern
which was established was that the counties and county districts
would try to arrive at some common front and would then seek
some *modus vivendi* with the AMC. At the same time it was
recognised by everyone that reform was impossible if a body with
the status of the AMC stood out. Under a common and obvious
threat all the associations united.

On the basis of their agreement to consult, the associations
prepared a memorandum for Jowitt. This was presented in
mid-1943 at a time when post-war planning had got under way.
It was becoming clear that many of the welfare and other
services planned for a 'reconstructed' Britain were not to be run
locally and indeed many services seemed likely to be taken away
from local government. United by this, the associations claimed
that the 'present proposals to redistribute services were ill-conceived.'
There seemed to them to be no co-ordination between the
proposals of the central departments affecting local government:
in education, for example, or in the health service. There
had been many inroads into local functions. On these grounds
the associations called for a Committee of Enquiry into local
government.

The answer to this was in line with earlier government statements.
There was enormous political pressure to set up the new services
which had priority over the reorganisation of structure. A
comprehensive enquiry would take too long and was therefore
impractical. With each department and all the political parties
clamouring for the new services, the government had no alternative
but to get them set up as quickly as possible.

Such an attitude did not make the associations feel any more secure.

Within a few days, a motion appeared on the Order Paper of the
House of Commons in the names of some prominent representatives of
the CCA.

that this House, whilst recognising that changes will be
required in the structure and functions of local government
in order to meet the consequent reorganisation of local services,
is determined to maintain the full responsibility of elected
local representatives and thus to preserve the vitality and
administrative efficiency of our democratic local institutions.

It is doubtful if this activity by the associations had any real effect.
They were, after all, agreed upon very little. The agreed that local
government should not lose services but in this they were not
successful for post-war government plans were carried out along these
lines. They were agreed that regional government was an evil, but
Jowitt himself appears to have lost interest in this at an early date.
They were formally agreed that a high-powered Committee of
Enquiry was necessary but, in the CCA, there were elements who
were by no means convinced that this was a good thing. Of the
two major associations, the CCA had the most to lose from any
comprehensive enquiry since it was felt that virtually any reform
would be along the lines of an increase in the territory of the towns.
Applications by individual towns for extensions could be spun out
but 'once and for all' measures promised big losses for the counties
in a very short time. Some far-sighted members may have seen that such
a procedure was equally likely to reduce the number of county
borough islands in counties but since all previous change had
been in the direction of enlarging these islands, it is hard to blame the
doubters. Britain was and is increasingly urbanised.

The associations were in a dilemma. Among the leaders there was,
as has been pointed out, an awareness that reforms were necessary for
the future well-being of local government. It was also true that they
contained member authorities who were threatened by even the
mildest reform. To abandon them would have been to stir up a
campaign against the leadership and therefore they had to
emphasise the benefits of their own particular form of administration.

For the associations the second phase started when the Local
Government Boundary Commission was announced in mid-1944. By
this time no one seriously feared a complete overturning of the
structure. The government had assured them of this in many ways. When
they met the Minister it was explained that the Commission was being
set up because the government expected a large number of proposals
for boundary extensions from the County Boroughs and that, rather
than dealing with them by Private Bill legislation, it would be more
satisfactory to take them all together. There was no question of their

considering functions or any new type of patterns.

Of all the associations, the CCA was probably happiest about the suggestions. The remit which was suggested for the Commission certainly rejected the scheme for a one-tier system and it was very close to the original memorandum which the CCA had put up.

Many members of the AMC were suspicious but, on the whole, this body also felt that its members would gain by the arrangements. In spite of the call for a Royal Commission, there had been a fear that the government might decide the principles of local government centrally and then apply them without consultation. At least this arrangement avoided that danger.

In the event the difference was resolved happily. The special sub-committee of the AMC decided to press that non-county boroughs should retain their rights under the 1933 Act. On the occasion of the debate on the White Paper all Vice-Presidents were circularised with a letter asking them to press this point among others. At the committee stage of the final Bill an amendment was put down by Sir Geoffrey Hutchinson QC (as he then was) to repeat the terms of Section 301 of the Act of 1933. This was finally withdrawn but a government amendment was inserted that the county council or Minister in changing any boundaries 'shall have regard to any representation made by the council of a county district included in the area in question'. The position of the small boroughs with ancient charters was to some extent safeguarded when the Minister accepted an AMC amendment.

... nothing in this Act shall prejudice, alter or affect the rights, privileges and immunities of any municipal corporation or the operation of any municipal charter.

The point of this example is that it shows clearly the divisions within the AMC. It shows the way in which they organised themselves and finally it illustrates that, in an appeal to ancient lineage and the established way of doing things, those authorities which might have been regarded as anachronistic even by members of their own associations, were on strong ground. It is significant that their point was conceded without too much of a struggle.

There are one or two general points which can be picked up from this point. First it is clear that the initiative for local government reform came from central government and not from local government itself. It was Whitehall that considered the quality of administration to be unsatisfactory. The second point is that there was virtual deadlock between the town interest represented in the AMC and the county interest represented by the CCA and the district councils associations. They had opposing proposals for the future and they perceived each other traditionally as enemies. There seems to have been little willingness to come together.

The situation at the end of the war is more or less as one would have predicted. There had been an attempt to make a radical change in the structure following the upheaval of values during the war. Such an attempt was a challenge to the position of important members of the local government world. Even though there were members of each local government interest who saw the need for change, they had to keep their members behind them. In view of this built-in opposition, central government, which was responsible finally for the running of the administration, decided that it was better to have a series of adjustments to boundaries (incremental changes) and to meet the inadequacy of the old system by removing services which it could not carry out and by subjecting others to close central control.

The Associations and The Local Government Boundary Commission

The coming of the Boundary Commission brought a lull in delegations and joint meetings, but it did not mean that all activity ceased.

In accordance with the different interests which have already been described inside the AMC different proposals were made to the Commission. Ordinary, medium-sized county boroughs pressed quite straightforwardly for extensions, and the larger non-county boroughs asked for their status to be raised. Both of these endorsed the case for a one-tier system of local authorities which had been put forward by the Association in 1942. The big county boroughs like Manchester were, on the other hand, attracted by a two-tier solution in which areas like their own would, with the addition of nearby urban areas, be continuous counties. This sort of scheme brought strong protests from authorities which saw themselves being swallowed up. The small non-county boroughs had never taken to the 1942 report and, against the formal position of the AMC, they were protagonists of the two-tier system. Thus, conflicting demands to the Commission came from different members of the Association. This controversy came to a head when the County Boroughs Association, with all its members also members of the AMC, sent a memorandum to the Commission pressing it to establish a one-tier system in this country in so far as this was possible. The annual conference of the Association for 1946 met in this threatening atmosphere and passed two resolutions:

> that this conference records its deep concern at piecemeal
> legislation which is removing the powers and responsibilities of
> municipal authorities and reaffirms its faith in local
> government based on democratic principle.

and

> that having regard to the minister's address the conference requests

General Purposes Committee of the Association, as a matter of
urgency, to give further consideration to the existing structure of
Local Government in the light of recent and pending legislation
and to report thereon, with recommendations, to the Council of
the Association.

The second resolution is a reference to the speech made by Bevan at
this conference. This and the general orientation of the Boundary
Commission seemed to be in the direction of a two-tier system. The
problem of the conurbations was coming to the fore and the
solutions which were being considered were nearly all in terms of
two layers. On the basis of these trends the committee was effectively
being asked to look again at the 1942 AMC policy statement
which outlined a one-tier system. The county boroughs could be
expected to be hostile and it was clear that the non-county boroughs
were behind their second resolution.

The resulting report overturned the policy of the Association.
It rehearsed the arguments for large and small areas of administration
and declared

the further conclusion to which the above examination seems
to lead is that in suitable cases a two-tier (or perhaps in some
cases a three-tier) system should be considered which would
embrace existing local authorities whether counties, county
boroughs, non-county boroughs, county districts and parishes.
The arguments for an adoption of the two- (or three-) tier system
which are specially relevant to the Association may be set out
as follows:
(a) it would allow large areas for major purposes;
(b) it would preserve the identity of all boroughs and while
    county boroughs affected would give up some of their
    powers they would, through their representatives, secure a
    voice in matters of common interest;
(c) it would secure an efficient system of local government
    capable of performing functions which are now being taken
    out of the sphere of local government.

The report went on to consider the distribution of functions for each
tier and concluded that rating should be the function of the second
tier. For a transitional period, members of the upper tier should be
elected by the lower tier councils.

The effect of this report was to cause a split in the Association. The
county boroughs could not be expected to accept this quietly and made
use of a clause in the constitution of the AMC which has never been
used before or since. Clause 2(2) states that 'whenever any clash
between the interests of the county boroughs and non-county
boroughs occured, the matter which has caused this clash shall be

dropped and the Association shall not take any part in it.' At the meeting called to discuss the report, a majority of the county boroughs (not including the largest ones such as Manchester, Liverpool, Leeds and Birmingham) voted that such a clash had taken place and it thus became impossible for the meeting to discuss the report and consequently to support any memorandum on these lines to the Boundary Commission.

The county boroughs and non-county boroughs were now openly opposed. The county boroughs had sent their own suggestions to the Commission withou consulting the AMC and the same county boroughs had prevented consideration of the General Purposes Committee's report. The Commission itself expressed some surprise that evidence should be given separately from the Association itself but, in answering, the Secretary of the county boroughs had assured them that:

The Association it (the council of the County Boroughs Association) represents is the only local government association capable, as a result of practical knowledge and experience, of expressing views upon and dealing with the merits of the County Boroughs system of government.

There was an equivalent report from non-county boroughs. They had suspected that there was to be a move by the county boroughs and had met before the full Association convened to decide strategy. At a subsequent meeting it was decided to request the Commission to let them state their views indicating that they believed the two-tier system to be the most satisfactory. Having received an invitation they then (in December) submitted a memorandum which shared many points with the earlier report of the AMC General Purposes Committee. It recommended that the second tier should be directly elected although transitionally its members might be appointed by the lower-tier authority.

The division was to bedevil the operation of the AMC and, indeed, the discussions on local government reorganisation for a very long time. It is significant that it was the county boroughs which were able to hold up matters. Any government which was particularly anxious to reform local government on two-tier lines would have had the support of the CCA, the UDCA, and the RDCA. In addition, a very large proportion of the AMC, the largest county boroughs and the non-county boroughs would have been in support of such a plan.

The event which questioned the whole one-tier approach was the second report of the Local Government Boundary Commission.[5]

For the CCA this report was something of a vindication. It was, therefore, to be expected that they should welcome it. This approval was not complete since they deplored the recommendation that education itself should go to the 'new county boroughs' but on the whole they were happy. They accepted the suggestion that highway functions could be performed by the 'new county boroughs' provided that they had the resources of highly trained staff and equipment. The planning proposals were acceptable provided the lower-tier authorities were regarded as agents of the counties and not as autonomous units.

The district councils' associations had mixed reactions to the report. The 'urbans' welcomed the two-tier plan but objected to the idea of substituting one set of District Councils for the existing split of urban and rural. The RDCA felt that they were not concerned with the report.

As far as the county boroughs were concerned, their Association sent a submission to Mr. Bevan regretting that the Commission had gone outside its terms of reference and that it had seen fit to suggest the strengthening of the two-tier system. Once again it was argued that the county borough system was the most democratic and the Minister was reminded that he himself had said that this was not the time for major reform. The county boroughs clearly felt that it was now they who were threatened by any major reform and not the rural areas. The AMC and the non-county boroughs were not committed.

The appearance of the report called for some comment by the associations as we have seen and also some consultation among them. The AMC made the first move and called a joint meeting on the 1 May 1948. After great delays this was convened on 9 December 1948 and to it the AMC submitted a memorandum. The general lines of approach of the Commission were unacceptable and the appointment of a Royal Commission was demanded to look into:

(1)   the place of local government in the modern state;
(2)   the future structure of local government;
(3)   the functions to be exercised by local government;
(4)   the future relations of local and central government.

What lay behind the recommendation was yet another outcome of the old split between county boroughs and non-county boroughs within the Association. The effect of this split and the earlier invoking of clause 2(2) was that the Association as a whole could not comment on the report in any positive way. To have done so would have involved a conflict of interest between the two types of member. As matters turned out the county boroughs were more effective than their smaller colleagues in forming the AMC's reply. The idea of a Royal Commission was theirs. It seemed virtually the only method of achieving the drastic changes which the desired and it was also a delaying tactic against the sorts of alterations which had been

recommended by the Commission. The Non-County Boroughs
Committee was not at all happy about this. In a letter to Sir Harold
Banwell, the Secretary explained that, in the first place, his committee
was in favour of the two-tier system. In addition, to appoint a
Royal Commission might very well lead to the 60,000 limit, which
had been recommended for the 'new county boroughs', being
lifted to a much higher figure. There might be a general deterioration
in the position of the non-county boroughs and the counties might well
use the time during which the committee was sitting to withdraw
delegated powers from them and to consolidate the case against them.
Despite this strong feeling, the AMC declared for a Royal Commission
at their meeting with the other associations. Ther could be no
doubt which faction was the more important within the AMC.

Unlike the AMC the other representatives meeting in December
1948 accepted the Commission's report. None of them had any use
for the idea of a Royal Commission although they agreed to go back
to their associations to air the point. It became clear at this meeting,
and indeed it had been clear before, that the other associations were
thus much closer on the future structure of local government. While
the AMC wanted a delaying tactic because of the weakness that the
split had caused, the CCA decided that the only way forward
was for it to unite the others to press the government for a scheme along
the lines of the Commission's report. Along with the other
associations, it therefore resolved that they had no desire to see
discussions proceed on the basis of a Royal Commission but would
rather continue meetings of the associations on the basis of the
controversial report. This decision, reached by the General
Purposes Committee of the CCA in January 1949, was reported to
the AMC. They in their turn were under considerable pressure from the
Non-County Boroughs Committee which officially welcomed the
Report of the Boundary Commission in January. A special sub-
committee took the view that, since non-county boroughs might suffer
by a long delay, the government should legislate to prevent changes in
the balance of power between the counties and the non-county
boroughs before an investigating body had been established.

At a meeting of the four associations in March 1949 the following
resolution was passed, the AMC abstaining:

that it be recommended to the associations that, for the purpose
of the present conference, discussions of the problem of local
government reform
(a) on the basis of a Royal Commission be abandoned;
(b) be continued on the basis of the 1947 report of the Local
    Government Boundary Commission.

This outcome marked a slight weakening in the rigidity of the AMC.

They indicated that they were not wholly committed to the Royal Commission idea and were quite able to discuss the 1947 report. A reason for this weakening seems to have been the growing obviousness of the fact that this proposal was not practical in the political climate.

Almost as soon as tentative agreement had been reached the Minister announced the dissolution of the Boundary Commission.

This left all the associations in something of a quandary. It was by no means clear what the government intended to do in the long term. Some members of the AMC believed that comprehensive legislation would be produced by the government after the election. There was no real indication of this. What was clear, however, was that any boundary extensions would now require the old procedure of Private Bill legislation which was both costly and time-consuming. In 1949 it was calculated that the cheapest form (unopposed private legislation) would cost at least £600 and with so many county boroughs bursting their seams on to so many unwilling counties, the cost would run into many thousands. There was a further tactical point which was made by many county boroughs. During the time of the Commission's investigations the claims of the county boroughs had been moderate and realistic. A quite different bargaining situation now arose. In pressing for boundary extensions they would have to argue against the counties and both would submit inflated claims in the hope that some compromise might be reached in the long run. It was felt that counties would now point to the more modest claims previously made in any discussions during the process of the Private Bill.

This section may be summed up by noting the reactions of the associations to the Local Government Boundary Commission's second report and to its dissolution. The associations had lined up for or against the second report on the basis of whether they liked or disliked two tiers. The AMC called for a Royal Commission in order to appeal to a neutral body with even higher status than the Boundary Commission. Later that Association realised that the alternative to change by the Boundary Commission was no change at all. The raising of the lower population limit for county boroughs might make it even more difficult to gain this status. Thus they eventually co-operated with the others in an attempt to retain the Commission. The fact remained, however, that each association worked to a rather narrow definition of what was in the interest of the strongest members. The CCA saw the second report as a way of maintaining county government. The demotion of most county boroughs to 'most purpose' status would save the problems of rateable value and planning which beset the counties.

1952-55

The dissolution of the Commission gave the AMC the opportunity to stop the embarrassing discussion of reorganisation. The counties on the other hand were keen to pursue the subject so that they could follow up the advantage which the Commission's recommendation of the two-tier system had given them. We now move into a period when the associations, or some of them, tried to work out a new structure. The recognised that reform would be necessary at some time, because of the facts of overspill and the anomalies in the sizes of authorities. For the CCA and its allies there was a clear advantage in trying to bring in reform while the two-tier ideas of the Boundary Commission were fresh in people's minds.

They were to have very limited success. In spite of several letters asking him to name dates for a joint meeting, Banwell was unable to make any satisfactory arrangements. The CCA's Parliamentary and General Purposes Committee therefore decided to seek a conference with the district councils associations which were nearer to its point of view in any case. The representatives of the AMC would of course be invited to participate.[6] By this time it was, however, clear that it was going to be almost impossible to reach agreement. This impossibility became confirmed when, in their February meeting,[7] the CCA General Purposes Committee laid down the basis for their discussions with other associations. This was to be:

(a)   the existing two-tier system;
(b)   that existing county boroughs of over 100,000 should retain their functions;
(c)   that other county boroughs should become county districts;
(d)   that county districts should be regrouped so that the minimum size would be 10,000;
(e)   that county districts with over 100,000 population would be able to apply for county borough status but that extensions to attain this should not be permitted for a period of fifteen years after the passing of the reform Bill;
(f)   County Districts with over 60,000 population should be given a considerable measure of delegated powere including primary and secondary education.

Although the AMC disliked this seizing of the initiative they agreed to attend a meeting on 29 March. Once there, they questioned the propriety of demoting any county borough without an enquiry and demanded that the figure of 100,000 should be reduced to 75,000. On this point the CCA indicated that they were prepared to talk. Furthermore the AMC and the UDCA co-operated to demand that full delegation should be given at 35,000 and not at 60,000. This first figure reflected the hand of the 'urbans' rather than the AMC who had always been more realistic at this level. There had, however, been some informal negotiations going on between the UDCA and the Non-County Boroughs Committee. As a result of this, on the same day as the four associations' meeting, they published a report which recommended that all boroughs over 60,000 should have major powers conferred directly upon them as of right. Between 35,000 and 60,000 they could have these powers if the Ministry found them to be efficient.

The AMC was not at all happy with the way the talks were going. It was felt that they were being manoeuvred into an endorsement of two-tier government and that the activities of the Non-County Boroughs Committee might force them into this. They had certainly pressed the AMC to enter into discussions on the subject of local government reform much against the judgement of its leaders.

The year 1951 saw the gradual breakdown of relations between the associations on the question of reorganisation. In the previous July the CCA had put forward a memorandum as a basis for discussion. It recommended the two-tier system. In an attempt to bring along the AMC the level at which county borough status could be granted would be 75,000. It further suggested that any county district affected by a county review could appeal to the Minister and that, if two or more districts were amalgamated, the status of the resulting district would be that of a non-county borough if one district was a non-county borough. All these were points which had been pressed by the AMC often under the influence of the Non-County Boroughs Committee. The exception was, of course, the endorsement of the two-tier system. In answer to this memorandum the AMC pressed for a one-tier system, for 50,000 as the necessary population limit for borough status and it also demanded that the county review should be carried out by an independent tribunal. This was, of course, totally unacceptable to the CCA and the AMC knew it. It was a delaying tactic pursued partly because the AMC was in an impossible position and also it appeared certain that a General Election was imminent. The leaders of the Association hoped that after the election the chances might be more favourable. The CCA, on the other hand, were keen that they should have their point of view established while political circumstances were not too hostile. Thus the four associations' meeting in October 1950 (where the AMC's objection were not accepted) was used to meet the claims of the UDCA who objected to a population minimum for county districts. This did not mean that they did not try seriously to keep the AMC in. They did so partly be some concessions and partly by informal contact with the Non-County Boroughs Committee which wanted the debate on reorganisation to come to a successful conclusion. The first few months of 1951 dragged away with meetings of the four secretaries getting nowhere. Then in September 1951, a statement was put to a joint meeting and the AMC was asked to react. Again the impending general election was pleaded as a reason for not acting immediately. In November, however, the associations met again and the AMC offered to submit a new memorandum on its views.

When this came it served only to deepen the split. The AMC took exception to the idea that the meetings had been really concerned with the future of local government. In their eyes it had only been a 'holding' operation. They claimed that in the beginning they had explained that they regarded certain questions as fundamental: questions such as functions, finance, conurbations and relations with central government. None of these had been discussed and the Association could not agree that they had reached a long-term solution. The essential difference between the associations now appeared to be that while the boroughs wished to have a thorough-going review of the whole situation, the other were for a patch-up job.

This had the effect of completely stopping discussions. In an attempt to salvage good relations the Secretary of the UDCA approached the AMC to ask them to put forward their own scheme for local government reform in detail but when this arrived it really said no more than the 1942 report. In a letter to Haslam of the UDCA[8] Banwell wrote:

> The sub-committee have asked me to say that their preference is for one-tier local government. Where such a system is not practicable or desirable they recognise that there may be a need for a form of two-tier government. This is subject, of course, to a satisfactory allocation of functions and powers between the types of authority.

In other words, the AMC saw the political situation as conducive only to short-term reform along two-tier lines and was determined to do nothing to help it along.

This was a virtual breakdown of relations between the AMC and the other three associations. The latter, who wanted to put pressure on the government for a reform which would preserve the existing system in broad outline, decided to meet together to present a report. In the last few meetings they had already conferred once or twice before meeting the AMC but now they had declared their intentions formally to co-operate.

From June 1952 the three remaining associations started to meet. In addition the National Association of Parish Councils, which had for some time been trying to make its voice heard, was invited to put forward its views on the place of parish councils. Although not very important politically, it had a nuisance value which pointed to its being included. As representative of the very smallest local units it might make things very embarrassingly politically, given the British cultural penchant for the localness of local government. In any case they were committed to the two-tier system.

The first meeting of the associations took place on 4 June. In December, a meeting was arranged with the NAPC on the basis of an agreed document and, after a certain amount of discussion over functions final agreement was reached.

Meanwhile the AMC had not been sleeping. It had used its Parliamentary contacts to publicise its one-tier proposals and even more to spread the idea of a Royal Commission. The 1952 Conservative Local Government Conference had a paper presented to it which largely put the AMC position. When the CCA heard about this and tried to put in one of their own they were told that it was too late and they should try for next year. Similarly, Mr. Peart (Labour, Workington) put down a motion to 'call attention to the need for local government reform and the setting up of a Royal Commission to conduct an investigation.' Needless to say this was against the spirit of the three associations' agreement which had stated:

the existing forms of local government have proved themselves to be not only satisfactory but also so flexible in essentials as to be capable of mutation and evolution without the necessity of any alteration of structure. (para. 7)

The Parliamentary motion was obviously inspired by the AMC. The Secretary of the CCA acted immediately and wrote to MPs who were known to be sympathetic to the county cause.

But relations between the two sides had not completely broken down. The report which was finally accepted by the CCA and the district councils associations was submitted to the AMC for its approval.

When an answere came in June it was not friendly:

We cannot recommend the contents of the County memorandum as a satisfactory solution of the difficulties of local government. It does no more than offer suggestions for the readjustment of existing areas and perpetuates the frustration of the present system. It gives no consideration to what functions an elected council should perform and what a suitable unit of local government should be to perform these functions.[9]

and again: 'Functions, areas and finance must be considered at one and the same time.'[10]

The AMC returned to the old charge that a thorough investigation alone could solve the problem which included the 'artificial severance of urban and rural communities.'

The reply repeated the Association's position on the two-tier system and returned to the idea that all-purpose authorities should have

a minimum population level set at 50,000. On the specialised question
of conurbations:

> We do not believe that the conurbations present such a serious
> difficulty as is sometimes suggested. Community of local
> interest is most marked in many of the areas of large
> population. We see no reason why the same basic principles
> which are applied to the rest of the country should not be
> applied to those areas with such limited modifications as to the
> extent of the areas may make necessary in regard to certain
> functions.

In May 1954 a meeting was held with the Minister who at that time
was Harold Macmillan. The AMC made it clear that their position was
backed by all classes of authority in membership: only twelve
authorities had voted against the final report. There was a clear
confrontation (on paper) between the counties and county districts on
the one hand and the boroughs on the other.

To the divided world of local government the Minister put three
questions. First, what was their attitude to local government finance?
On this the AMC wanted a return to the situation before 1929 when
agricultural and industrial properties were derated. They suggested
that the idea of assigned revenues should be examined but they were
against a local income tax. On the first and last points at least the
other associations were with them . Second, the Minister asked them if
they had thought about the redistribution of functions. None of the
associations said more than appeared in the four associations'
memorandum, but the AMC commented that hospital administration,
valuation for rating and possibly the distribution of gas and electricity
should return to the local authorities. Finally, the Minister asked about
structure with special reference to arrangements in the conurbations.
Both sides took up their traditional position on one- and two-tier
systems. The AMC agreed that, in the case of a two-tier system, the
upper tier should be something in the nature of a joint committee.
They further argued that 50,000 was a good size for an all-purpose
authority. This was of course, a return to the old 1888 figure and
appears as a kind of a bargaining counter against the CCA figure of
75,000 rather than as a serious suggestion. In addition there was an
intriguing detail with regard to parish councils. It will be remembered
that the three 'two-tier' associations had asked the National Association
of Parish Councils to join them after being pressed by that
Association to receive a deputation. In the same way the AMC also
consulted the 'parishes'. Where the latter had been concerned to see
that their councils might survive the process of any reform and had
suggested that areas added to a borough should retain their parish
councils, the AMC went one step further. It saw no objection to the

parish system being spread to existing borough areas as well as being retained in ones which had already been rural.

Macmillan did not seem keen to initiate moves on reorganisation. His part in the discussions with the associations had been mostly to ask questions. He had made no real indication of his own position other than making it clear that he thought the present local government structure basically sound and he did not contemplate radical changes. In effect, the whole matter was referred back to the associations.

Part of the reason for this may have been that a general election seemed to be fairly near and, as had been the case with many other ministers responsible for local government, his major concern was elsewhere; in this case it was with housing. Five months after the meeting in May, Macmillan had gone to Defence. A man on his way to the top could not crucify himself on the cross of reorganisation; building houses was easier.

This meeting marked the last phase of the period when local government itself tried to work for a new system. It failed because of the divisions within its own ranks and also because reform was a topic which could only be faced by central government if it thought that there would be a fair hope of success and if it could be sure that there would be a reasonable payoff.

The 1958 Act

The new Minister, Duncan Sandys, brought in an entirely new situation. He forced the pace between the assocations and agreement was reached on limited reform. He had, of course, made it clear that no class of authority was threatened.

By the end of the year all discussions with interested ministries on the function of the tiers after reorganisation had been completed. The publication of the White Paper started a new round of discussions within the associations and between them. As had happened in the past a whole series of meetings was convened within the AMC. The County Boroughs Association met as did also the Non-County Boroughs Association but in addition there was a meeting of small boroughs (around 15,000) and of the ten large non-county boroughs which had been specially singled out for promotion by the Local Government Boundary Commission. The large boroughs were beginning to show signs of exasperation with the smaller ones and were even threatening to say so openly and to take a concerted and independent line with the government or with the new Commission when it was appointed. They were persuaded against this by the Secretary of the Non-County Boroughs Committee who pointed out that to do this would be to present a disunited front to the other side. Thus the secretary of this committee was playing a role similar to the one played so often by the secretary of the parent body. The final attitude of this association to the White Paper was expressed by a report approved by a special meeting.[11]

On the important question of conurbations it was felt that the Minister should consult all the local authorities affected before designating an area as a conurbation and that each conurbation should be looked at in itself alone. There should be no general solution for conurbations. The meeting was asked not to pass a resolution critical of the 125,000 population limit for one-tier authorities in conurbations since the Minister had been in favour of a much higher figure. As far as county boroughs in general were concerned the AMC felt that decisions on status should be made, not upon the basis of the existing population, but upon the population which was planned. In the case of non-county boroughs, the Association was in favour of county reviews being done by some independent body such as the Commission and not by the counties. They were in favour of direct conferment of functions as opposed to delegation even of the compulsory type. Thus the AMC as usual had to face internal dissension over its policy. The most important cause of this was argument over the minimum population sizes and the principles of delegation.

In January 1957 the County Councils Associations produced a similar document. It warned of the dangers and inconvenience for the surrounding area of creating new county boroughs and complained that the Minister seemed much keener to demote or amalgamate counties than to reduce the status of the very small county boroughs. The Association objected to the Minister's suggestion that there might be more than the six conurbations recognised by the Registrar General for the Census and argued that, apart from the case of Lancashire, these units should all remain under the control of the relevant county. Finally, it rejected the idea of a minimum population for county districts and declared that the idea of conferring certain existing functions of county councils on county district councils was ill-conceived. These last two proposals seem to be very closely connected to the relations between the CCA and the two county district associations. They seem to be the two sides of a deal between the associations. At an earlier stage of the negotiations representatives had provisionally agreed to the idea of the direct conferment of these functions. Long before the White Paper had been issued, however, the CCA had considered the matter and the members had not been able to agree. Instead they suggested a system of compulsory delegation. In their memorandum to the Ministry the association pointed out that the agreement of the representatives to a policy had never bound their respective membership. In all, it was felt that the scheme which the

White Paper put forward could be made to work if satisfactory agreement could be reached on the questions of finance and functions.

In May 1957 the White Papers on finance and functions were published.[12] The reactions of the local authority associations could have been predicted. The CCA was reasonably well satisfied as was the RDCA. The UDCA expressed some disappointment that the principle of direct conferment had been rejected but the Annual Report of the Executive Council was prepared to suspend judgement upon it until it could estimate the effect on its members. The Annual Conference of the Association in June took a different view. It rejected the White Paper since it did 'not constitute a satisfactory basis for the future allocation of functions between county councils and county district councils'. As for the AMC, reaction was virtually confined to the non-county boroughs, especially the small ones who objected strongly to the population limit of 60,000.

Another source of borough complaint came from Middlesex, in that the White Paper on functions envisaged the continuation of the two-tier system here. The leadership of the Association felt strongly that this was an issue on which the government would not give way. After a meeting with representatives of the Middlesex boroughs, however, it was agreed that the Association should press for Middlesex to be treated in the same way as the rest of the country. In all the associations there was one common complaint, sometimes stated but always in the background. The White Paper on functions was different from that on areas and structure in that it was not the product of an agreement between the associations and the ministries concerned. Many felt that the associations had not been given a full opportunity to represent their case and, indeed, the AMC objected to this in their first comment on the document. What appears to have happened is that there was a great deal of talking between the associations and the ministries concerned individually, but before the White Paper no overall picture appeared.

With all three of the promised White Papers now published the interested parties began to test whether negotiations could improve their own positions. The sub-groupings within the AMC were first. At a meeting on 29 May 1957, the Non-County Boroughs Committee resolved

that the non-county boroughs of England and Wales express profound dissatisfaction with the proposals outlined in the White Paper which, if implemented, would materially effect the status of non-county boroughs reducing them to the rank of agents of the county councils; in particular they protest against the refusal to confer powers directly on them; and press that the statement on paragraph 6 of the White Paper, that the government are anxious that larger responsibilities should be entrusted to the District Councils, be implemented in full. They ask the AMC to take all possible steps to ensure that non-county boroughs can continue to take part in local government which is compatible with their tradition, experience and record.

A flood of letters replying to the request for comments by boroughs forced the AMC to adopt the points of this resolution at a special meeting of the associations in June 1957. It was widely felt in the associations that those boroughs under 60,000 would actually lose powers and in particular the cases of food and drugs and weights and measures were mentioned. These and other points were pressed by Sir Harold Banwell at a meeting at the Ministry with senior officials on 11 June. It was agreed that two or more authorities could make joint applications for amalgamation and simultaneously for county borough status. But the Ministry officials could not agree that the safeguards against demotion of a county borough within a conurbation should be the same as that for one outside. In conurbations the inter-relations between authorities was much more important. It was agreed, however, that the Local Government Commission should have the power to create a new county council. As for the figure at which maximum.delegation was to be possible, the AMC again put forward the figure of 50,000 as against that of 75,000 for the CCA.

Apart from the higher figure for complete delegation, which seems to have been largely a tactical point, the CCA was happy with the White Paper on functions.

It is interesting that the pattern of alliances now changes. Whereas before the AMC had stood alone against the rest on the question of one tier against two, they were now jointed by the Urban District Councils Association and those two together pressed against the counties and the 'rurals' for a lower level for full delegation.

The Commons debate on the White Paper brought out the local government interests in full panoply. But the situation did not change much. Some of the attack was directed at the counties. Mr. Mitchison, the Opposition spokesman, criticised the proposal that the counties should be able to carry out the review of district boundaries,[13] and in a similar vein, questioned the difference between 'direct conferment' and 'compulsory delegation'. This latter arrangement was now demanded by the CCA and seemed to have the blessings of the government. The Opposition spokesman argued that 'compulsory delegation' only served to keep control in the hands of the County Councils whereas what was really wanted was as much devolution as possible. In answer to Brook's argument that the White Paper held out hope of this to the lower-tier authorities, Mitchison pointed out that there were only fifty-five county districts over 60,000 and that they alone would get anything out of the White Paper. They would become almost the 'Most Purpose Authorities' of the Local Government Boundary Commission. Authorities with a population below 60,000 would in most cases lose powers. This objection to the principle of delegation was voiced by many Labour MPs, some of whom had connections with the AMC.[14] One Labour speaker was David Griffiths of Rother Valley.[15] As he was the President of the UDCA, it was hardly surprising that he should also question the population limit of 60,000. In this he was joined by a Conservative, Sir Ian Orr Ewing, who spoke as President of the RDCA. Most of the criticism was in terms of the vested interests of various types of local authorities and only a few speakers seemed to lift their eyes up to the hills. George Lindgren summed matters up when, in winding up the first day's debate for the Opposition, he said:

> From the way some people talk and have spoken even in this debate, including the Minister, one would think that the present general structure of local government is sacrosanct. The average citizen does not care twopence whether he lives in a County Borough, an Urban District or whatever we call it. He wants services . . . provided at a reasonable cost.[16]

He went on to spell out another argument, fairly common on the Labour side but hardly ever expressed by Conservatives, that local government services are national services applied locally without the government relinquishing responsibility for their quality. Conservative *legislation* had often embodied this sentiment.

The Local Government Commission

In the two years before the 1958 Act it had been clear that there would have been reform had the local authorities wanted it and had they been able to present a united demand to the government. Apart from the divide between the AMC and the rest, each organisation had its own malcontents. This was important in the AMC since if this group had gained greater influence, there could have been a real move for reorganisation. Each association and each faction fought for its own narrowly defined interest. No one in the world of local government could propose a formula for reform which would be acceptable to all. The interests within local government could not reconcile themselves to structural reform and initiative had to come from the outside. As it came from a conservative bureaucratic source, its proposals were for incremental not radical changes. The instrument of change was to be the Local Government Commission.

The general reactions of the associations to the Commission seem to have changed at various points. At first all were apprehensive. The AMC had always demanded a Royal Commission and there were elements who felt that the present arrangements were very much of a second best. Both the CCA and the AMC had members smaller than the suggested minimum and they were soon to get complaints that their case was not being given weight by the Commission. At a very early stage[17] the County Clerk of Ely wrote to the CCA Secretary reporting that a Commission had shown great interest in the subject of case loads: especially in the fields of health and child welfare. The inability of small authorities to provide specialist officers with a job was obvious. There was much uncertainty about the way in which the Commission would proceed and the CCA pressed for county councils to have an equal right with the Commission to put proposals to the Minister. This Association seems to have pursued a very rigorous policy at this time, even encouraging its members to be represented by counsel despite the preference of the government for a more informal approach. Its attitude suggests that, having got the Commission to operate what seemed to be terms acceptable to its side, the CCA was determined to press the advantage and to lose as little as possible.

It would be a mistake to suggest that the associations took a direct part in the fights of individual members for their existing status or for extensions. In the first case the leaders were aware that they had members whose minuteness was a drawback in putting the case for their type of authority as a whole. Especially in the AMC there were strong demands from these smaller members that their positions should be safeguarded. There is little doubt of the informal interest of both associations but, apart from seeing that the procedure was fair, the authorities were left to fight their own battles. The very nature of the Commission's way of working and that of the Minister's inspectors also excluded this tactic.

The case of Rutland illustrates this point best of all. During the long (and incredibly successful) struggle there was virtually no correspondence with CCA headquarters. The Secretary sent a personal note expressing admiration for the gallant fight but some very senior figures in the organisation were known to be on the side of the Commission.

The problem which faced the county authorities was that they were bound to lose territory if a local government Commission existed at all. It was largely as a result of county borough demands that the Commission had been set up. The government knew that the absence of such a body would have led to a flood of private Bills for extensions. It was inevitable that county councils should feel that they were being discriminated against whenever they lost land and it was difficult for them to see that the real question to be answered was the extent to which the demands of the county boroughs and larger non-county boroughs could be held back. The Commission was an instrument of modernisation despite the fact that its role had been written in a traditional script.

There can be no doubt that from the beginning the AMC was reasonably satisfied with the working of the Commission and the CCA increasingly apprehensive. The reason was, of course, that the orientation of the Commission had become much more sympathetic towards the towns. The AMC gradually forgot about its earlier demand for a Royal Commission to look at local government *de novo* and the CCA began to cast around for new ways of influencing events. One of the interesting sidelights on this was that the relations between the Commission and the CCA were never as cordial as they had been with the old Local Government Boundary Commission. Trustam Eve and his colleagues had been much less inclined to extend the county borough principle. On the contrary, with their 'most-purpose authorities' more power would eventually have gone to the counties. It is a reasonable guess that lower-tier units, even when they are specifically created with more powers than their predecessors, nearly always lose to the centre and the upper-tier authorities. The Local Government Commission, though vested with more powers than the Local Government Boundary Commission, was less adventurous. The effect of their recommendations was to build up the county boroughs where the demand for change was most keenly felt, thus allowing short-term change.

From the beginning of 1963 there started a definite move on the part of many county clerks to have the remit of the Commission reconsidered. There was a certain hesitation at first in that such a move, while it might well prevent more county boroughs from being created, would probably also undermine the position of the smaller counties. For this reason the CCA did not openly subscribe to this move. Indeed the Secretary, Dacey, went out of his way to dissuade the ring-leaders. Having come under particularly heavy pressure in Lancashire and Cheshire, in May 1963 Dacey eventually wrote to the Permanent Secretary, Dame Evelyn Sharp, informing her that his Association wanted to re-open discussions on local government reform. He repeated the argument that a population of 100,000 was too small for a viable single-tier authority and called to witness first the recent report of the Royal Commission on the Police where the effectiveness of small forces had been questioned, and second, the recommendation that new towns should be planned for populations of around 150,000. All this he placed in the context of what he saw as the Commissions' creation of new county boroughs whenever possible.

A meeting between the CCA representatives and Dame Evelyn was

convened on 10 May 1963. She made it clear that there was no question
of the review being stopped in mid-stream and pointed out that what
was happening was the righting of an imbalance which had lasted for the
twenty years in which Private Bill legislation had almost come to a
standstill. She agreed that 100,000 was too small for a county borough;
the present London boroughs were larger, but on the other hand, it
was not possible to rethink the structure of local government at that
time. It would be done at some time but this time was not opportune.

Clearly this would not satisfy the Association. It took the whole
affair further when it met the Commission on 23 July. This meeting
was held after the expression of strong feeling in the Association that
small county boroughs were being more gently treated than small
counties. Hence the Commission was asked to consider that, while the
figure of 100,000 was settled by Parliament, it was challenged by
other considerations. Secondly, it was argued that, while the
Commission had, in the view of the Association, over-emphasised the
question of efficiency, it seemed to have disregarded the participation
of the electorate and the question of the convenience of the unit.
What was wanted was an undertaking that the Commission would regard
counties with a population of 100,000 as not at risk, or that it would
agree to apply the same standards to counties and county boroughs
alike. In reply the Association was asked to name a minimum population
for counties but it shrank from such a dangerous commitment.

It was inevitable that there should be some pressure on the CCA from
small counties who were liable to disappear. The AMC too were
pressurised by the non-county boroughs but their targets of criticism
were the counties who carried out reviews threatening the status of the
smaller boroughs. It was true that several county boroughs were
demoted but, on balance, the existence of the Commission brought the
towns more benefits than losses. Only a few small county boroughs or
non-county boroughs lost status.

From the summer of 1964 onwards the CCA pressure to end the
Commission was intense. This dissatisfaction with the Commission
and with the acceptance of the 100,000 population minimum led the
counties to be somewhat more realistic about their own minimum
sizes. In the autumn a report prepared by the Secretary and a
committee of clerks suggested that the Association should accept a
high but unspecified minimum for counties; a thing which they had
previously avoided. To this top tier would be given the functions of
traffic control, transprot, police, fire, ambulance and education.
There would be two sorts of second tier; the first, with a population
of from 20,000 to 100,000; the second from 100,000 to 240,000. This
was an important development in the recognition that it was necessary
to move to larger sizes.

The CCA met the new Minister (Richard Crossman) in February putting their points to him and emphasising especially the need to raise the minimum population of county boroughs to around 200,000 and urging a new look at the Local Government Commission. It was at this meeting that the Minister first expressed what was to be a constant theme: the split between the town and country. At least this was a move from the usual hedging reception. Even with this, however, the members of the deputation got the impression that the Commission was to continue. Crossman himself had said at the TCPA dinner[18] that there would be no fundamental changes in local government structure for the next ten years. In the background, however, other things were happening.

On 4 November George Brown, the Secretary of State for Economic Affairs, made a statement in the House of Commons outlining the government's plans for the regions.[19] The significance of this was immediately recognised by the associations. Mr. Brown gave the standard reassurance. Unassured the associations consulted. At the Labour Party's Local Government Conference, the *Guardian* reported Mr. Brown:

> It was not fundamentally the government's purpose to change the structure of local government although he thought there was a great deal of room for fundamental change.
>
> the Labour movement would find him on its side as soon as it adopted elected regional government as its policy.[20]

This was an interesting observation. Mr. Crossman was more cautious. He held out the prospect of quick decisions on the Commission's proposals and of later, but much later, changing its terms of reference. Eventually, however, Crossman set up the Royal Commission and the Local Government Commission was ended.

All the associations finally welcomed the Minister's proposal. For the AMC however the smile was forced. Most of its county borough members were distressed at the prospect of 'their' commission being disbanded. This meant the suspension of any extensions for a long time. The CCA was delighted.

The whole period from the setting up of the Local Government Commission had clearly been a time of change. People became more used to the idea of larger authorities and started to be aware of the needs of the conurbations. Even in this atmosphere, however, the associations still worked hard in their own interest. The types of authority most threatened by the Commission fought for its abolition when, faced by the facts of demography and the needs of planning, it took more and more territory away from the counties. Alongside the associations the Ministry and central government showed a preference for incremental change in the 1958 Act and it was the

Commission itself which, through its working, painfully and almost
unconsciously began to suggest new forms of local government.
Finally, these new forms came from the world of planning and from
other developments near the world of local government. Even the
local authority associations had to recognise the danger of *ad hoc*
authorities and centralisation. New values seemed ready to replace the
old ones.

The Redcliffe Maud Commission

In the time between the appointment of the Royal Commission and its
report, the main activities of the associations with regard to reform
lay in preparing written and oral evidence for the Commission. In this
they accepted the idea of larger units. It is also notable that the
associations stuck to their old ideas about structure and, given the
possibility of a radical and almost certain change in the local
government system, did not come together to provide some united
solution to the problem which had been with the British system for the
last thrity years at least. It was not simply that the AMC took a line
which was unacceptable to the CCA, RDCA, UDCA alliance. Once again
the AMC was split. The county boroughs and the non-county boroughs
did not see eye to eye and the split this time became quite open.

Most of the evidence from the associations came in October 1966.
The AMC official view which was supported by the majority of the
non-county boroughs in the membership was in favour of an entirely
new pattern of local government. For the first time the Association
came out in favour of a two-tier system. On the one hand there would
be 'Provinces' which would cover very large areas as the name might
suggest and which would have only such powers as would require such
a wide scope. Structural planning was the obvious example. The
minimum size of such provinces would be half a million. Alongside
these provinces would be the local councils which would run the bulk
of the local government services. No exact sizes were given for these
authorities. Presumably there would be a range and presumably the
majority of them would be based on existing small and medium-sized
towns since this scheme was being pressed by the Non-County Boroughs
Association. These local authorities would be brought about by the
merging of towns with the surrounding countryside. The AMC agreed
that there were parts of England where such a pattern might not be
ideal. In sparsely populated areas and in the conurbations there might
be a need for special arrangements but as a general pattern the AMC
argued that this was the best. True to its tradition the AMC did not
give an indication of the average size of these local units. When pressed
during the oral evidence it indicated that there would be a wide range

depending on local circumstances.

The County Boroughs Association opposed this evidence. They had been outvoted when the matter was discussed within the AMC itself and they publicly dissociated themselves from it when it appeared. They argued for a pure one-tier system on much the same pattern as that laid down in the 1942 proposals. There was a great deal of charging and counter-charging between the County Boroughs Association and the AMC and when the AMC finally came to give oral evidence to the Commission in April 1967 it was thought necessary to include in the Association's delegation the Chairman and Secretaries of both the County Boroughs Association and the Non-County Boroughs Committee.

The CCA, as in the past, supported a two-tier solution. In this case, however, it was the existing type of two-tier system that was proposed. The top tier would consist of enlarged counties rather than the AMC's privinces. Where the AMC gave little power to this top tier the CCA placed the key services at this level.

Thus there should be forty to fifty upper-level units. Naturally they would be smaller than the existing Economic Planning Regions. At the lower lever there were to be units which would perform the functions looked after by the county districts. Their sizes should range from 40,000 to 150,000. In the case of the very largest towns there might be exceptions but for practical purposes this was a proposal for a continuation of the existing county system without the very smallest counties and without the majority of county borough islands. In addition, of course, there was to be a rationalisation of the district structure. The recommended upsetting as little as possible the existing boundaries where the AMC was in favour of tearing up the map.

The RDCA and the UDCA evidence was not materially different from that of their county allies. The UDCA took a major ideological step forward when it agreed in the memorandum that bigger could mean better. Both Urbans and Rurals tended to concentrate on the idea that services should be carried out by the smallest authority capable of undertaking them but once again this was in line with the representation of their interests. For the Rurals there was a move towards the acceptance of larger authorities when they accepted, in their evidence, a minimum of 30,000 for districts. One could, indeed, say that the acceptance of larger units was a common feature of the documents presented by all the local government associations. This was, however, the only real move which the associations made from the positions which they had taken up before the Commission had been appointed.

The first reactions of the CCA and the AMC to Maud were rather guarded. Both put out statements but needed more time to find out how the reform would affect their own members. The AMC accepted the Report with reservations. The minimum sizes of the unitary authorities seemed too high to them. There was also an objection on the part of some large towns which were to be part of conurbations that they would be swallowed up by this arrangement. The CCA, on the other hand. felt that some of the proposed unitary authorities were too small to work effectively. They also suggested that, contrary to the AMC line, a second tier should be brought in to look after the needs of local democracy. They also suggested that, in at least some areas of the country, such a second tier was necessary for efficiency also. At the very least this should be recognised by setting up district committees of the unitary authority to deal with the services to sub-divisions of the unitary authority. Another CCA reaction was that the boundaries of conurbations should be more tightly drawn.

It was the district council associations which reacted most quickly and definitely against Maud. The Report appeared during the annual conference of the RDCA and within two days a decision had been made to mount a £40,000 publicity campaign. The central feature of this was a strip cartoon which followed the outrageous behaviour of a pompous Centralising Bureaucrat: 'R.E. Mote'. An immense amount of the Association's effort was put into this.

We may interpret the first reactions of the associations in much the same way as they have been interpreted before. In the case of the two largest associations there were some counties and county boroughs which had come very well out of Maud. For other large authorities, especially counties, the Report proposed dismemberment and other forms of dislocation. For the district council associations the situation was clear. Any reform along unitary lines would mean that they would all disappear. There was no question but that these associations were opposed.

The stage thus seemed set for the reincarnation of some form of the old 'non-borough alliance' and in November it came into the open. On 14 November a letter was sent by the CCA on behalf of the RDCA and UDCA and themselves to Sir Matthew Stevenson, the Permanent Secretary at the Ministry of Housing and Local Government.

It is clear from this letter that the associations were not completely agreed. It was the associations for the district councils which argued for a two-tier system for the country. The CCA was more cautious:

> Whilst acknowledging the advantages of this type of authority
> they consider that, in practice, some positive arrangements are
> required to ensure the participation of more elected members
> in the administration of these services. For this purpose,
> the County Councils Association have suggested that each unitary

authority should decentralise administration of selected appropriate functions to district committees.

The CCA seemed to indicate in this letter that it might be persuaded that the Maud type of authority was the best. On the whole, however, it had decided to come together with the other two to put forward an old style two-tier scheme. Another point of interest is that the letter spoke of 'progress so far made' suggesting that there was more to come. No further communication was sent to the Ministry perhaps because the CCA preferred to maintain this rather ambiguous stand or because the election brought in a Conservative government committed to a two-tier system. Whatever the reasons for the action or lack of action the proposals in the letter were very close to those of the district council associations. The top tier should have a minimum population of half a million while for the second tier the limits should be 60,000 to 100,000 'and in some areas with a higher population'. This position was a long way from the pre-Maud position of the district councils. The top tier authorities were to be responsible for planning, police, fire, transportation and principal highways (including traffic management), education, personal health services, social work services, water supply, consumer protection, refuse and sewage disposal, major housing development and overspill housing. Some aspects of these various services were still under discussion among the associations but the outline was clear.

What did all this amount to? Briefly the battle lines had once again been drawn up by the associations. The same groups had come together for the same reasons. It was true that the levels of minimum population had been considerably raised. Maud had raised everyone's sights. But on the subject of one tier versus two tiers, the position was still the same. Although some counties had come out of the Commission's report quite well, others, including the very influential counties of Lancashire and Cheshire, were to have their areas very badly cut about. In Warwickshire and in the South East there were problems too. The problems of these counties forced the CCA into an ambiguous position. Once again straightforward attachment to the status quo and self-interest can explain the reactions of the parties. It may also explain the background to the exercise on behalf of Cheshire County Council which showed that a Maud system of local government reform would cost £200,000,000. There was, of course, no estimate of the cost of not reforming.

It was not only through public relations and contact with the Ministry that the 'two-tier' associations fought. The County Councils Association and, much more vigorously and openly, the RDCA exerted pressure upon the Conservative Party. The Tories had organised a series of meetings with Conservative local government people all over the

country to hear their views on Maud. To these meetings Rural District
Councillors turned up in great numbers and helped to create the
impression of implacable opposition to Maud. As far as the Conservative
Shadow Cabinet was concerned they were largely successful. This
pressure was connected with the R.E. Mote campaign. It was noisy
but, as an indication of the length to which the Association was
prepared to go to push its case, not really successful. There were
no obvious payoffs and it did not get a great deal of coverage in the
national press. Probably the quieter and more insistent pressure from
county councils was as effective.

On the other side of the local government divide the AMC was
occupying its traditional position and it had its traditional problems.
It has already been pointed out that there was opposition to the size
of the units proposed since such a system would wipe out a large
number of existing county boroughs but this was a matter for
negotiation. The commitment which the AMC had to a unitary system
and in general its support of the county boroughs against the claims of
the surrounding areas made negotiation with the other associations
pointless. Although there was some suggestion of a joint approach
before the November 1969 letter of the three associations, it was in
character that the AMC worked on its own. Or almost on its own.
In December 1969 the AMC came together with the National
Association of Parish Councils to support Maud. As far as the latter
organisation was concerned it was more likely that this lowest tier
of local government would survive under unitary proposals than
under a two-tier system. If there was to be a second tier then the point
of the parish or local councils would be lost. Certainly they would not
run any services or be anything other than a sounding board.

At the September 1969 conference of the AMC when the Maud
report was discussed many non-county borough representatives spoke
in favour of a two-tier system as opposed to the acceptance of the
unitary principle in the draft memorandum before the conference.
The Chairman, Alderman Frank Marshall of Leeds, explained that the
general purposes committee thought the best interests of the
association would be served 'by accepting the logic of the unitary
authority'. The hand of the county boroughs was pretty apparent.
There were a number of motions hostile to this one-tier idea and, in the
event, one which had been prepared at a meeting of the Non-County
Boroughs Committee was carried by a majority of 146 votes to 97.
It asked the AMC council to consider introducing further flexibility
into their final memorandum by proposing to the government that in
some appropriate parts of the country there could be a two-tier system.
When this proposal came to be discussed by the AMC council, the
county boroughs yet again won the day and the non-county boroughs

were out-manoeuvred by a combination of leadership (favourable to the county boroughs) from the platform and lack of any leadership at all on the part of the rest.

When the White Paper on Local Government Reform appeared, in February 1970, the AMC reaced with a long, detailed critique in which it deplored the government's shelving of the idea of provincial councils. Finally in November 1970 the AMC put out yet another plan which although differently phrased in no way deviated from its previous argument in favour of a large number of unitary authorities. The only new departure was that the Association suggested for the first time certain boundaries for the new authorities. The main reason for the appearance of this report seems to have been the return of a Conservative government. Since it was committed to a two-tier system it was necessary for the AMC to propose a structure which would best fit its interests. The result was a system of fourteen provinces and 132 most-purpose authorities, with a population of 150,000 or 200,000. The upper tier was to have control over such services as strategic planning, further education, special schools, the fire and police services and so forth. Commenting on the scheme, the CCA pointed out that it was almost identical with the AMC evidence to Maud which had been rejected. The important point about this exchange is not the detail of the proposal and counter-proposal but that, in spite of all the discussion that had taken place and the agreement of almost all that reform was needed, the major local government interests had not changed. The positions were the same as they had adopted in the 1950s.

When the 1971 White Paper was published the reactions were again predictable. The CCA was satisfied since the new counties were largely based on the old counties. The AMC deplored the fact that efficient and democratic towns would disappear in what looked like a county administrators' solution. But there was little root and branch opposition from the boroughs. Perhaps it had simply become clear that this was a plan which the Conservative government had decided to put through. Perhaps it was that the AMC no longer had much energy left for a fight. Instead it combined with the urbans and rurals to press for more district powers. In the course of the Parliamentary debate, then, it was the alliance that applied most pressure on the government through their vice-presidents and other spokesmen. They were successful in having the proposal for joint planning staff scrapped and in obtaining local planning and development control for the districts.

Conclusion

Looking back over this long and repetitive story some themes stood out.

Local government interests and especially the AMC, because of its internal divisions, moved very little from their original positions in formal terms. It is also interesting that there was an unchanging pattern of alliances except on those occasions when the powers of districts were being discussed. It seems to point to a real antagonism between the larger towns and the smaller urban and rural districts. The town was perceived to be encroaching upon the countryside. The county boroughs, with their experience and manpower, could maintain a line as against the non-county boroughs whose interests were much closer to the 'county alliance'. There was, however, a change in atmosphere. The leaders of the associations did, in the later years, recognise that change was necessary and were less inclined to defend the indefensible among their members. A great part of the impetus for this change came from the fact that central government became determined to change the system in one way or another. In the years immediately after the war the first priority for the government was the provision of essential services. Few would argue that this provision was perfect by the 'sixties but the basis was there and it became possible to look at other things. In particular it became possible to look at the organisation of the structure in the knowledge that it had not done particularly well in the running of these essential services. Everyone was aware of the massive central intervention which had been necessary to get programmes through and in no service was this clearer than in planning. Central government teams had been responsible for regional planning since the beginning of the 'sixties and were working more and more closely with local planning departments. With a focus on the whole of local government for their particular type of local authority it was easier for leaders of the associations to see the need for reform. In very large measure this explains the relatively sudden collapse of opposition to reform once a determined government had shown that it meant to overhaul the system.

NOTES

1.   *'The Leader'* Correspondence, 25.7.1872.
2.   *Anonymous Empire.* Pall Mall Press, London, 1963, pp. 3-4.
3.   These have been mentioned in earlier chapters. Principally the Labour government adopted reform and efficiency as one of the symbols.

4.   See p. 39 above.
5.   Ibid.
6.   25.1.50.
7.   6.2.50.
8.   7.5.52.
9.   para. 7.
10.   para. 8
11.   12.12.56.
12.   Cmnd. 161/1957 and Cmnd. 209/1957. HMSO, London.
13.   House of Commons Debates, vol. 874, col. 941.
14.   Ibid., co. 970.
15.   Ibid., co. 991.
16.   Ibid., co. 1007.
17.   20.4.59.
18.   2.12.64.
19.   House of Commons Debates, vol. 701, cols. 228-230.
20.   29.3.65.

4   THE PARTIES AND LOCAL GOVERNMENT REFORM

Some Themes

A key reason for the failure to reform local government was that until 1966, no political party would take it up. In the section which follows the reasons for the parties' inaction will be examined.

In British parliamentary government it is important for the success of a legislative proposal that it should have the support of one of the main parties. All but a few Private Members' Bills are destroyed. In the case of an important piece of legislation like the reform of local government, it is unthinkable that it should be dealt with by a private member. The situation, therefore, is that reform could not be accomplished other than by a major piece of government legislation. This imples the support of the party in government. Any hesitation by this party to take up local government reform presents an insuperable obstacle.

Local government reform is not a vote-winner on any party's platform.[1] Very few electors know or care much about local government. The ignorance revealed by the research done for Redcliffe Maud is an indication of this.[2] Nor is it something which could be expected to rally the party faithful. They tend to be more interested in matters of national politics. So far from attracting votes, local government reform is likely to alienate people. A large proportion of party workers in Britain are connected with local government. Some of them are councillors and key figures in their local organisations. A change in local government structure may mean an end to the interests of a lifetime. They will certainly use the party meetings to protest against this. Others may have hopes of becoming candidates. For the rest of the workers, there is a much keener awareness of local authorities and affection for these authorities than exists among the population at large.[3] The low polls at municipal elections show clearly that it is only the party enthusiast who takes an interest in local government.[4] Since it is this group which is most involved with existing local loyalties it is also precisely this group which may be offended by a plan for reorganisation. The man who has run the City Labour Party or the County Conservative Association will have a knowledge of and affection for the city and county. He may feel bitter that the unit which he serves is threatened. This applies to people who are not party functionaries but whose influence is important for the local organisation. Trade unions, Womens Institutes,

Rotaries and all kinds of other organisations are territorially based upon the existing local government units. An upheaval for the latter may well mean an upheaval for the former and the man and women who comprise them are the party workers who do the canvassing, make the speeches and run the national elections. Even if they are not party activists they are the sort of people with whom party activists come in contact and who, for them, constitute public opinion. Local party supporters and their colleagues in community organisations are likely to feel threatened by reform proposals. The party which attempts reform will make few new friends since the advocates of reform tend to be intellectuals or administrators, and can make enemies out of their most valued supporters.

There is, too, the uncertainty caused by such a measure. A change in the boundaries can mean that wards or constituenceis which have been safe suddenly become marginal or even hopeless.[5] Even when it is not clear that the move will be disadvantageous there is doubt, for it is impossible to estimate the effect of reform on party strength in the whole country. Such a situation is clearly not one which recommends itself to people who are used to thinking in 'incremental' terms. The party manager is used to maximising his vote in the existing situation. It is unlikely that the 'leap in the dark' will appeal to him.

There are other and less obvious reasons why political parties should not be attracted by local government reform. It is not clearly a 'political' decision in the way in which some issues call for 'political' decisions. The values inherent in local government reform are not ones which are usually appealed to in the propaganda of either party. Such obvious appeals as improved social welfare, increased employment, law and order are not obviously advanced by reform which is, in essence, administrative and therefore peripheral to the issues which the parties see as being central to their philosophy.

To say that the reform of the machine is peripheral implies that the parties believe that the tasks which they wish to perform can be performed within the existing machine. Whenever it is clear that this is not so, the path of reform is made clear since the institution in question is seen to deny the value which is upheld by the party. Thus it was easier to reform local government in 1835 since the old corporations were found to be corrupt and were centres of reaction. When the Whigs came into power the aim of sweeping away the old corporations was central to their programme. It was part of the ex extension of the franchise. In the twentieth century the major parties held power in unreformed local government. They contained large groups, for most of the time majorities, who believed that the existing machine was adequate. Where its areas were too small, *ad hoc* arrangements such as the regional Water Boards could be set up which did not threaten the existence of local government although they could curtail its power. For the party it is important that the service be carried out since this what gets votes. It was only when there came into power a party which declared efficiency as one of its planks and projected an image of a new, dynamic group of administrators, that old institutions seemed at risk. The values of the party were now very much at odds with the maintenance of the *status quo*.

There is a final theme which runs through the account to be given. It has been said that the institutions of local government did not deny the principles of the parties in an obvious way. Part of the reason for this was that the parties, like local government, were part of the system of British institutions. When one part of a system changes there is change elsewhere because many of the assumptions held in that part operate elsewhere. Just as the parties had to support the values of democracy, local involvement and decentralised administration which were symbolised by the local authorities. Parties found it difficult to reform local government because an attack on it appeared to be an attack on these values.

Party Organisation for Local Government

It has often been suggested that national political parties have only recently come into local government. There are many who deplore the development as a move towards centralisation and ideological rigidity. They blame the Labour Party which began to contest seats at the beginning of the century and thus forced the Conservatives to enter the contest as well. It is certainly true that there was a burst of political activity by the Socialists before the First World War but national parties have been interested in local government elections since the nineteenth century. It has already been pointed out that the measures of 1835 were politically motivated since the unreformed corporations controlled votes for seats at Westminster. Similarly, the Birmingham Caucus under Chamberlain is a famous and important piece of British political history.[6] Professor Hanham's study shows however that party involvement was older and more widespread than is commonly acknowledged.[7] Towns like Liverpool and Leeds had vigorous contests based upon national politics in the eighteen-forties and 'fifties.[8] During the nineteenth century there were high points of political controversy in local government when particularly contentious issues were debated by many authorities. Towards the end of the century most of the controversy moved to the School Boards in which once again elections were conducted on partisan lines in many places.[9] Anglican Tories and Dissenting Liberals had quite different pictures of the policies which the Boards should pursue. There can be no doubt that the national political parties were present in nineteenth-century local government as in the twentieth-century. In both periods they were there for the same reasons. Certain policies could only be carried out if *local* government was in the hands of like-minded men. Party control of councils was used not only to implement policy but also to see that magistrates and other key figures were elected according to their party loyalties. In the earlier part of the century the town clerk had also been appointed on that basis. In London the party managers were by no means unaware of this. Among the Conservatives in Peels' day Bonham collated the results of the local elections as an indicator of popular feeling.[10] When Gorst became principal Conservative Agent he actively encouraged the entry of Conservaties into the Councils.[11] National parties have, therefore, been involved in the local government system for a long time, andy any proposal that there should be a change in the system was bound to be regarded rather cautiously by the party managers. It is significant that the 1888 Act was introduced at a time when party controversy in local government was rather muted as compared to the situation on the School Boards.

By the end of the nineteenth-century the national party organisations had recognised that local government contests were of importance for them both as prognosticators of national elections and as a way of keeping the machine in trim for fighting constituency battles. Another factor influenced their thinking along these lines. Where in the nineteenth-century most of the decisions taken by a council did not fit clearly into a pattern of national legislation, in this century local government came to carry out functions closely controlled by national legislation. Education, social welfare, house building and planning were all local government services subject to a greater or lesser degree of central review and inspection. The outlines of the policy which was to be followed were laid down by national legislation and the performance was monitored by Whitehall.[12] In many cases the parties differed in the emphasis which they placed on different policies. In a few, such as comprehensive secondary education, council house rents and the question of direct labour departments, there was serious disagreement. Thus local policy was also national policy and a party entered local government because this was the only way in which its policies could be implemented.

In all these ways, then, the national political parties were involved with the existing local system. They were involved because local personnel were also officers or workers for the parties. They were involved because local elections reflected the fortunes of the parties and finally because of the importance of local government for the implementation of national policy. The effect of this interpenetration was that individuals concerned with local government formed a strong pressure group within each of the party organisations.

This 'presence' of local government within the parties took various institutional forms. A study of these may illustrate the difficulties which parties had in pursuing local government reform. The best-known example is the appointment of Members of Parliament and of the House of Lords as vice-presidents of the local government associations. The AMC did this and it is common for an organisation to retain MPs in order to represent its interests when the need arises. Those members who were sympathetic to local government associations had the benefit of a well-informed and efficient machine which could help them in their work. More than this, the form of local government which the MP had in his constituency had a special call on his attention.

The converse arrangement is one in which the parties formed groups within the local government associations. In an informal sense this operated in all the local government associations but it was most clearly developed in the AMC where in 1968 the Conservatives used their voting strength to unseat the Chairman, Sir Mark Henig, who was a Labour Councillor in Leicester, and to replace him with a Conservative – Councillor Frank Marshal of Leeds.

The practice of party members coming together before the meetings of the associations was started by Labour. In 1945 Labour delegates to the AMC were convened to go through the agenda of the meeting. There was, however, no suggestion that decisions taken in this preliminary meeting at the national Labour party's headquarters were binding. The meeting, which has continued up to the present day, had more the character of an exchange of views. There are some issues on which all Labour and Conservative members speak with one voice in their respective organisations. This is not invariably the case. What can be said is that the parties on the AMC organised party votes for *positions* or committee membership on these bodies rather than whipping the members to vote on *issues*.

Both the parties hold local government conferences. The Conservatives were in the lead here with their first Annual Local Government Conference in 1947. It was not until 1956 that a regular conference of this sort was held by Labour but before this date there had been national meetings of Labour groups starting with a conference in Nottingham in December 1945. Thus, the parties organised meetings where local government pressure could be placed upon them.

The parties also showed their concern for local government by the publication of journals and by the activities of parts of their national organisations. The Conservatives published *The Councillor* from 1946 onwards and, in addition, many pamphlets on local government matters in the *Town Hall* series. Labour has also published a newsletter for Labour Groups which since 1965 has been called

Partnership. Both Research Departments have had sections dealing
with local government matters since 1946.

Finally, the controlling councils of both the main parties contain
committees or sub-committees which deal with local government
matters. In the Conservative Party the National Advisory Committee
on Local Government was set up in 1946. It consists of three local
authority members from each of the regions together with one
representative each from the six largest cities. This body meets once
a quarter. Since 1955 the Labour Party National Executive Committee
has had a local government section of the Home Policy Sub-Committee.
By contrast with the Conservatives its membership is drawn mainly from
the nationally elected NEC rather than consisting of local government
figures. Various Members of Parliament are co-opted into this
committee including the chairman of the Parliamentary Labour Party's
committee on local government. In addition, people representing
various types of local government are co-opted. In the past there have
been extremely senior local government figures from large centres such
as Birmingham, Manchester and County Durham. These at least are
the members who attend regularly and the effect has been an over-
representation of the large boroughs. In the Parliamentary Party's
committee there is no attempt to balance out the various sorts of local
government interest. Members are free to join any committee which
interests them. Both the Labour and the Conservative parties are
organised in such a way that there is a great deal of inter-linking with
the local government system which makes it possible for local
government representatives to put pressure on the parties or even on
occasion to use parts of them as platforms for their own views.
It is, perhaps, significant that the part of the governing council of
the Labour party which is concerned with local government is not
as heavily representative of local government interests as is the case
with the Conservatives.

The Parties' Changing View of Reform

During the war there was a definite move towards reform. It was the
Labour Party which came closest to this. Its Central Committee on
Post-War Reconstruction set up a Sub-Committee on the Machinery
of Local Government under the chairmanship of Emmanuel Shinwell,
one of many such groups which were to formulate plans for party
policy and to produce a report for party approval. In July 1942 a
pamphlet on 'Local Government in the Post-War World' was produced
and in the next few months this was discussed in thirty-four
conferences all over the country. As a result of these conferences a
final document, 'The Future of Local Government', was produced for

the consideration of a national conference in June 1943 which was to
debate reports from all the sub-committees.

In recommending the report, James Griffiths of the NEC moved
the following motion which sums up the main points:

This conference recognises that the existing system of local
government based on county, borough, district and parish
units has rendered outstanding service, but holds that
conditions have now so changed that larger units of local
government are required for efficiency and economy, planning
and administration and for equitable distribution of cost and urges
therefore that —

  (a) new local government regions should be created in which there
      would be —
      (i) regional authorities;
      (ii) secondary or area authorities.
      The sites, boundaries and number of authorities would be
      determined according to the population, rateable value,
      administrative convenience and balance of town and country.
  (b) both regional and area authorities should be democratically
      constituted and operated. Both should be allotted appropriate
      tasks of local government with requisite financial and other
      powers.

The report had the approval of the NEC which, in effect, meant the
non-parliamentary leadership.

First, a radical change in the present system was being recommended.
In the course of Griffith's speech it became apparent that what was
being recommended was a system of about forty regions and 300
area authorities. As the Redcliffe Maud Commission was later to
point out, this was a considerable reduction to the existing total of local
authorities. In a time of crisis such as war, it is not surprising that
radical solutions were sought. When the crisis passed thorough-going
solutions also seemed to fade away. The second interesting point is
that they planned for a two-tier system. Morgan Phillips, the
Party Secretary, commented upon this. 'Let me give one or two
reasons which led us to reject the idea of a single all-purpose
authority . . . We must try to bring up to standard the differences
between town and country. We can do this by taking same services
and administering them over a wider area.' Phillips also commented
that the joint arrangements to which single-tier authorities gave rise
did not work satisfactorily in practice.

Finally, it is interesting that at this early stage the plan should
have been made with the intention of bringing together town and
county in one unit. As Griffiths said: 'The present boundaries and
present structure create a division between town and country which

is inimical to the best interests of the nation.'

It was this report which, of all those on many aspects of post-war policy, gave rise to the most heated debate. Even at a time in which the anomalies of the system were widely recognised, the defenders of the *status quo* were able to put up a stern fight. The hostile amendment which was put down against the Executive's report was rejected by 966,000 votes to 1,542,000. The report was accepted but, where most of the reports had not even had amendments put up to them, this one ran into serious opposition. When plans were actually put into legislative terms after 1945 this opposition ensured that the subject of local government reform would be ignored.

Given this situation it is not surprising that Labour did not protest too much when the Local Government Boundary Commission was set up. For those who believed that root and branch reform was necessary, this body was a second best. Its remit was only to rearrange the existing system which was far less than was called for by the official Labour party policy. In the debate on 15 February 1945 the Minister of Health (Mr. Willink) moved 'that this House welcomes the intentions of the government to preserve the existing framework of the county and county borough system of local government and the proposals for the establishment of a Local Government Boundary Commission.' The Labour Party spokesman described the proposals as 'timid and weak'. He pointed out that they cut across the policy of the Party but, having done this, the motion was agreed to. The main part of the debate was concerned with national and local government finance.

The Conservatives do not appear to have thought much about reform during the war years. After 1945, when they were in Opposition, there were several discussions at annual conferences. Labour, perhaps because it was the governing party, did not take up the subject at a conference until 1952 when it was in Opposition.

At the first Conservative Local Government Conference in 1947 a paper was given by Enoch Powell, then Head of the Conservative secretariat dealing with local government and health matters. Introducing him, the Chairman hoped that: 'as a result of a full and free exchange of views . . . we may be able, as party to make up our minds what can be done with local government structure.'

In short, there was no officially approved party policy as yet. Powell opened up certain themes but neither he nor any of the speakers who debated what he said were anywhere as specific as the Labour Party had been. The topic of one or two tiers, for example, was not touched on, neither did anyone give an indication of the range of sizes which might be appropriate for the future. It was clear, however, that the Conservatives had a different approach. A great deal of the discussion in the Labour Party has been about the efficient performance of services. The leadership, at any rate, had spent most of its time on this. Powell, on the other hand, said: 'Our object is first and foremost to obtain genuine local community areas and, having done that, let the rest of the local government structure upwards and downwards be built to fit them.'

Many speakers warned of the dangers of centralisation and recommended local government as a bastion against this danger. At the end of the debate no resolution was passed but there was a consensus in favour of the small authority and against centralisation. These themes were picked up by the main speaker at the conference, Col. Elliott, who was chairman of the Conservative Members Committee on Housing and Local Government. His whole address suggested that a root and branch reform would not be acceptable.

Speaking about the structure he said:

Firstly, it ought to be local. It has to be connected with some
area where, by tradition and history and modern practice it
can work as a unity, feeling its own corporate consciousness.

and again: 'bigness is the snare of local administration.'
These are themes which constantly recur in Conservative discussions of the subject.

At the second Conservative Local Government Conference in 1948 the subject was tackled in a more specific way. Two papers were given on alternative approaches to reform. Alderman Pike of Finchley, a London Metropolitan Borough, spoke on the one-tier system and Alderman Grimshaw of Hornsey Metropolitan Borough spoke as an advocate of two tiers. No conclusion was reached at the end of the conference. It was felt that both systems were necessary for different parts of the country. The papers do suggest, however, that there had been attempts by the local government associations to enlist the support of the party.

After these post-war years there is a tailing off in the discussion of reorganisation. Both the major parties were committed to arguments over topics which seemed more immediate. There was the controversy over nationalisation, the way in which Britain should be rebuilt and, closer to the debate on local government structure, the question of the National Health Service.

The Ministry of Health at that time was the department responsible for local government structure. Its Minister, Aneurin Bevan, was one of the most important figures in the Labour government and one who was regarded as a leader of the Left. It was in his period of office that the Local Government Boundary Commission reported and was dissolved. If we study Bevan's position it is easy to see why this should have happened. He was much more concerned with setting up the

National Health Service. He had an emotional commitment to this not simply because it was a very large scheme demanding all his organisational skills but because, such a service would mean that the poor would no longer have to suffer ill health.

It was to be expected that the Conservative Party would leap to the defence of the Local Government Boundary Commission when Labour terminated it.[13] The Commons debate showed this clearly enough but there was no specific approval by the Opposition of the Commission's proposals. In a paper prepared for the 1951 Conservative Local Government Conference, Walter Elliot described the Commission's suggestions as 'the most suggestive and reasonable recommendations recently brought before us,' and said, 'as a major step towards reorganisation we should re-establish the Local Government Boundary Commission and give it clear and precise terms of reference.' Elliot, who was an official Party spokesman, made no commitment to the precise proposals of the Commission. He agreed that many existing authorities were too small but he also said: 'we must build with what bricks we have . . . I am strongly in favour of county borough government where it is suitable and with the two-tier structure in the administrative counties. I abhor the idea of regional authorities which are only local in the sense that they are not national.'

Here at least he was at variance with the line taken by the Labour Party in 1943. On the other hand it was by no means clear what line the Labour party was now taking. In sacking the Commission, Bevan seemed to say that there was to be no radical change. No strong voices were raised within his party to remind him of the wartime policy. When Labour left office there was again no effort to reassume a radical line on local government reform. Given the scope of opposition for policy-making without the difficulties of implementation, this lack of a party line is significant. It illustrates how delicate the question really was.

There is a final point to be made about Conservative attitudes to the Local Government Boundary Commission. The proposals for 'most-purpose authorities' were welcomed by the County Councils Association because they represented, to their mind, an attack on the system of autonomous county boroughs. Counties, with some amalgamations, would have remained pretty much as they were. It is possible that the 'county interest' which is an important pressure group within that party, was able to ensure that this line would be taken. There is no doubt that the CCA was regarded as the most conservative of the Local Government Associations. When the Commission reported and at many other times there was regular contact between individual Conservatives and the CCA. When the

Redcliffe Maud Commission came to report there was to be a much
clearer intervention by the 'county interest' within the party and one
that was to have much more important consequences.

The next point at which reform came to be discussed was from
1955 until 1958 when the Act was passed setting up the Local
Government Commission. The responses of the parties were
characteristic of their previous positions. This Conservative measure
was one in which the principles of the existing structure were in no way
questioned. The Commission was confined to readjusting boundaries
and making a few demotions or promotions. Typically, the Labour
Party devoted most of the Second Reading debate to discussing the
financial provisions of the Bill and virtually nothing to criticism of
the structural principles.[14]

It was not long before the Conservative Party was in trouble with its
membership over the activities of the Commission. The most spectacular
case was Rutland where the smallest county in England was preserved
despite the Commission's recommendation of a merger with
Leicestershire. This is a particularly clear example of the importance of
the 'county interest' within the Party. The lobby in favour of the
retention of Rutland was largely an aristocratic and upper-class group.
In other matters this may not have been an asset but in this case it
certainly was. Towards the end of the Conservative period in office
other counties joined in the protest against the activities of the
Commission. Particularly notable were the activities of Cheshire and
Lancashire and intra-party channels were widely used.

When Labour came into office the internal pressure upon the
governing party came from a different direction but it was, if anything,
more intense. Again the reasons were straightforward. The plans of the
Commission were by this time more ambitious than they had been at
the beginning of their work. Many of them entailed the
amalgamation of Labour-dominated towns with suburbs and the
surrounding countryside in such a way that the Labour dominance
might be broken. A great deal of private pressure was brought to bear
on Richard Crossman, the new Minister.

Whether or not these vigorous protests, mostly from the boroughs,
had a cumulative effect, and played a part in the decision to
abolish the Commission, there is no doubt that Crossman decided that
the Commission was not an appropriate body for the work which had
to be done. His decision to appoint a Royal Commission fits in with
other aspects of Labour's orientation.

It was consistent with the difficulties of the parties that neither
Conservative nor Labour gave evidence to Maud. There had been a
number of attempts to get some discussion of reorganisation on their
respective local government committees but none of them had been

conclusive in reaching any kind of agreement. It was only when the report came out that positions began to be taken. Labour's general position was made clear by the Prime Minister, Mr. Wilson, in a statement announcing the report in the House of Commons. He accepted the report in principle, saying that there had to be larger units and that they had to embrace town and country.[15] The one-tier idea of Maud was also accepted. The equivalent Conservative statement was a great deal more tentative. Wilson saw the report as part of the general modernising process which was Labour's task. He had emphasised this approached since before 1964. Now that a thorough-going plan for reform was placed before him there was a good chance that he would accept it.

The Redcliffe Maud proposals were dealt with by both the main parties by calling a series of conferences in the regions. Within the Labour Party, first of all, the eight conferences were addressed by government speakers, including Anthony Greenwood, Arthur Skeffington, Anthony Crosland and Wayland Young. To them were invited Labour councillors but in addition there were representatives of the constituency parties. The effect of this was that there was much less of a concentration of the local government interest and consequently a greater probability that radical changes would be accepted. The party produced a discussion document, *Local Government Reform in England,*[16] which did not take sides on the actual type of the new structure but nudged the conferences in the direction of larger units. In the regional Labour Party conferences, there was quite strong backing for the Maud proposals from the platform. Only two of them were opposed to Maud. The West Midlands meeting was against the arrangements for the Birmingham conurbation both at the conference and later in a private delegation to Anthony Crosland. In the South West some worries were expressed about the proposal that Salisbury should go into the West Country. Generally, however, there was widespread support in the Labour Party for the outline of the Commission's proposals.

In January 1970 the NEC policy document, *Principles of Local Government Reform in England,* was published. It was based on the regional conferences and various written representations and it reflected the support for Maud which had been shown at these meetings. Its major deviation from Maud, a call for more metropolitan areas, reflected the power of the strong party groups in the big cities.

The situation in the Conservative Party was quite different. Significantly no discussion document was produced since the leadership had not made up its mind. In the course of the eleven conferences held by Peter Walker, the Opposition spokesman on local government, the most vigorous antagonism was expressed to the proposals. The organisation of these meetings was quite different from that in the Labour Party. Walker went to these conferences with an open mind. He did not try to steer the meetings towards one particular solution. There had been vigorous activity within the party against Maud. The R.E. Mote campaign of the RDCA was the most publicised part of this activity. Members of Rural District Councils were encouraged to express their views at meetings and the Conservative Party conferences were heaven-sent opportunities for their attitudes to be expressed. They were extensively used for this purpose. The CCA also added its weight against Maud with the result that Conservative local government appeared to be solidly in opposition to this type of reorganisation. Walker, who had started this series of meetings with a fair disposition towards the solution of the Commission, was forced to recognise that only a limited reform and a two-tier system had any chance of acceptance within his party. Probably the most important conference in this respect was that in the North West since there was such a high concentration of important local authorities. But the feeling was fairly uniform throughout the country. At the subsequent Conservative Local Government Conference in 1970 Walker was forced to take a clear two-tier line. But no definitive policy document was produced. The options were still open.

Broadly speaking, therefore, both parties included a range of views but the Labour Party came out in favour of Maud and the Conservatives were against it. At the 1969 Conference there were twenty-six hostile Conservative resolutions while for Labour only five parties put down critical resolutions.

Why was it that the two parties differed so radically on local government reform? For practical purposes this was the first time that such a split had come into the open.

It is surprising that the Labour Party should have accepted the reform so quietly. Any reorganisation which puts towns, especially big towns, together with the countryside, means putting at risk existing Labour domination. Its strength in the old areas and in the council housing estates would be more than balanced in many places by the union of middle-class suburbs and the countryside. Perhaps the reason why this particular line of argument was not put more forcefully was that, by the turn of the political tide, there were few councils in Labour hands at the time when the report was published. It is a common pattern in British politics that the party in power nationally loses support at the local level. Labour had been particularly hard-hit. In 1964 when they first came into office there were many Labour majorities in the boroughs. By 1969 this had fallen drastically. An important factor in the docility of the Labour Party may, therefore, have been the fact that the 'local government interest', in the sense of the councillors, was rather depleted. It certainly could not turn up in such massive numbers at the conferences which were held to discuss the proposals. Consequently the arguments of the councillors most likely to support the *status quo* would be outweighted by the constituency, trade union and other representatives who attended these meetings. Conversely, the proportion of councillors at the conferences might explain the stronger opposition by the Tories. They were the beneficiaries of the Labour downfall and thus there would be more Conservative councillors attending the discussions than would have been the case under a Conservative government. Nineteen-sixty-nine was a particularly good year for the Conservatives.

The second reason for Labour acceptance and Conservative hostility may be that these regional conferences were given more definite leadership by Labour than by the Conservatives. The government and NEC speakers who introduced the discussions were essentially on the side of Maud. Peter Walker had no such commitment and was prepared to be led by the feeling of the meetings.

Why were Labour leaders committed to the principles of Maud? It has already been pointed out that this commitment came out in the Prime Minister's statement to the Commons. Firstly, this was a Commission set up by the Labour Party and at a time when the government was unpopular there was strong pressure on the rank and file to keep quiet. Secondly from ministerial statements at the time when it was set up, it was clear that the Cabinet expected a radical solution. Maud was nothing if not radical and this mood fitted well with the dynamic and efficient image that the government wished to project for itself.

For the Conservatives the situation was different. Important symbols for them were the 'localness' of local government, the excellence of the existing institutions and such negative symbols as 'centralisation' and 'big government'. Both in symbolic terms and in terms of council seats currently held which were in danger, the Conservatives were more inclined to oppose the measures than was Labour. It it also true that reforms were bound to hit the rural interest hardest of all by 'contaminating' them with the towns. Finally, the Labour Cabinet at that time contained no one who had any particular commitment to one form of local government. Crossman, the Minister, was one of the few who had any local government experience. With a characteristic flourish it was he who set the Commission on its course and it was also characteristic that Wilson should give him his head to run policy in his own way.

We now turn to subsequent developments and first of all to the modifications of the proposals which were made in the Labour government's White Paper. Perhaps the most notable feature about it is just how much it agrees with Redcliffe Maud;

The Government differ only on the distribution of functions in areas
where there are to be two tiers, the application of the Commission's
structure in two parts of England, and certain aspects of the
proposals for local councils.[17]

There had been considerable pressure brought to bear upon Anthony
Crosland, the new Minister, for an extension of two-tier metropolitan
areas to other parts of the county. Tyneside, Sheffield, Teesside, Leeds
and the Preston-Leyland-Chorley complex sent delegations of Labour
councillors and officers. In their normal strength big city groups would
have been a powerful lobby. In the event only Leeds was chosen and
that for good planning reasons. Party pressure appears to have played a
minor role. In the course of the debate on the White Paper on
16 February, Peter Walker, for the Opposition, criticised the
government for its disguised centralisation but again he was extremely
cautious about the plans which he himself would adopt.

The Conservatives in Government

One of the surprises of the Conservative government was that Peter
Walker brought in proposals for reform so quickly. It was reasonable to
suppose that he would allow this measure to be crowded out by the
Parliamentary timetable. There was opposition to any reform from
those parts of British society which are most identified with the
Conservatives. The fact that he did not delay almost certainly had to
do with the image which this new administration, like its predecessors,
wanted to project. It was to be an 'efficient' administration. It was to
cut away all the dead wood and honour all its commitments. At the
same time the Conservatives had a different emphasis from Labour.
The 1970 Conservative manifesto stated:

the government in Whitehall is overloaded and as a result,
people in the regions grow increasingly impatient about the
decisions being made in London which they knew could be
better made locally . . . we think it wrong that the balance of
power between central and local government should have been
distorted and we will redress the balance and increase the
independence of local authorities.

It is difficult to decide whether this is an exercise in rhetoric or in
policy intention. On balance it seems more likely to be the former.
Certainly party statements outside the parliamentary debate did not
suggest that Labour was prepared to fight hard for its interpretation of
reform. It was significant, for example, that in his Fabian pamphlet
A Social Democratic Britain, Crosland (the Shadow Minister) did not
mention reform of local government as one of his socialist aims. He was
very well aware that the party was divided on the issue and as more

local government seats were won by Labour in 1971 and 1972 the split became important. There was hardly any discussion of the issue of reform on the NEC. This was almost exclusively a matter which was settled within the Parliamentary Labour Party. Thus even where a clear difference existed between the parties this did not represent a cleavage that divided all parts of the organisations.

In the passage of the Bill through Parliament various difference between the parties were raised. Party lines on local government reform were drawn in a way that had not existed before. At the same time one may doubt just how committed Labour was to some of the points.

One topic which was debated on the second reading was the question of two tiers as opposed to one and the related topic of provinces. John Silkin, who led for Labour, claimed that the one-tier — two-tier argument was a genuine difference between the parties. There was only one Labour member, James Johnson of Hull West, who was in favour of the two-tier system but this was hardly an issue which was burned into the conscience of the party.

The same comment can be made of the debate on provinces. Labour Parliament spokesmen attempted to amend the Bill so that counties were amalgamated into provinces or regions. This proposal sprang from a strong tradition within the party which has been referred to several times. It also sprang from a real concern with the situation whereby such services as the supply of water and health functions were being administered on a regional basis. Again, however, these points were not pursued with any vigour and they were probably of concern to few.

On the question of functions, Labour tried hardest to alter the provisions of the Bill relating to Education and Planning. For the former an attempt was made to put the services under metropolitan county control instead of the metropolitan district councils. The amendment was defeated. In planning, too, Labour was in favour of all the power being at the higher level. Their points were not, however, pressed too hard and they appeared to be happy with an assurance by the Minister that, where there was a conflict, the county solution would generally be given priority.

In these topics Labour showed a traditional concern, close to its championing of a one-tier system, for an increase of the scale of local government and a move to regionalism. Much less traditional and more in line with the fashionable politics of the day was its call for community councils in all areas. Labour was also concerned in this move to maintain towns with some semblance of separate identity.

Conclusion

The main British parties took up different stands on local government reform in the 1970s. Their reasons for doing so are not straightforward. Labour's adherence to the unitary principle largely depended on the fact that this was proposed by a Commission appointed by a Labour government, supported by the fact that few major figures in the party were concerned about the structure of local government. For their part the Conservatives were under heavy pressure from 'the county interest' and showed themselves to be more open to outside persuasion than was Labour. The Act which finally received the Royal Assent was close in substance to the County Councils Association scheme.

Only when a Labour government for whom the symbols of reform were important, came in did reorganisation become possible and reform was actually implemented by a Conservative administration that was similarly committed.

NOTES

1. A study of attitudes to local government reform in Edinburgh in 1966 showed that only 24% of the electors could name once councillor.
2. See vol. III, Research Appendices, pp. 141-151.
3. Clearly if party activists have to organise elections in local authority wards they are more likely to be conscious of the boundaries, names of councillors and functions of the authorities. In a Glasgow survey in 1966, 16% of the activists had heard of proposals to reorganise local government in Glasgow. The pilot survey for the electors' questionnarie showed that for electors this question was not even worth asking.
4. The GLC elections with turnouts of around 35% are by no means odd. If one compares this with turnouts of over 70% at General Elections the point comes out rather clearly.
5. This was brought home particularly clearly by the reform of London government. The LCC had been a safe Labour council but, with the addition of middle-class suburbs, the GLC became very marginal. The fact that Labour won it in the first elections in 1964 came as something of a surprise to everyone.
6. See D. Read, *The English Provinces,* Arnold, London, 1964, pp. 173-4.
7. H. Hanham, *Elections and Party Management: Politicians in the Time of Disraeli and Gladstone,* Longmans, London, 1959
8. See Ramsay Muir, *A History of Liverpool,* Liverpool University Press, Liverpool, 1907, pp. 309-15.

9. See Francis Adams, *History of the Elementary School Contest in England,* Brighton, Harvester Press, 1973, pp. 246-57.
10. See Hanham, p. 388, and N. Gash, 'F.R. Bonham', *English Historical Review,* LXIII, pp. 502-33, 1948.
11. See Hanham, p. 389.
12. See John A.G. Griffiths, *Central Departments and Local Authorities,* Allen and Unwin, London, 1966.
13. The Local Government Commission (Dissolution) Act, 1969, received the Royal Assent on 16 December 1969.
14. House of Commons Debates, vol. 579, col. 901-1019, 9 December 1957.
15. House of Commons Debates, vol. 784, cols. 1460-75, 11 June 1969.
16. The Labour Party, London, 1969.
17. Cmnd. 4276/1970, para. 9.

5 LOCAL GOVERNMENT REFORM: A STUDY OF STRUCTURAL MODERNISATION

In all the research which has been done on politics in developed countries, little attention has been paid to the modernisation of governmental structure. The changes in the class system, in recruitment patterns or in socialisation have been discussed but there has been little of value on institutions, an omission which is understandable reaction against the time when laws and institutions were virtually the only things studied by political scientists. *A priori,* institutions appear to be one of the most important factors influencing political behaviour and politics in general. This is not to argue that the formal arrangements exactly represent the way in which the system works, but they are the catalyst around which formal relationships develop. The fact that local government exists in Britain means that party workers have a power base other than their ability to bring out the vote at national elections. They have power over parts of the administrative system, and are able to make certain demands of central government which otherwise would be futile. An alternative to or an abolition of some part of local government would alter political behaviour and the power distribution in the United Kingdom.

It is difficult to define 'modernisation'. It may be cultural snobbery to associate this process with the movement towards a state of affairs which characterises modern European civilisation. Nevertheless, societies all over the world are beginning to show characteristics which first developed in European society. There is a tendency towards greater scale of the institutions and towards bureaucratisation. Certain types of problem become characteristic. Because of urbanisation difficulties of physical planning have to be faced. The state tends to take more part in social welfare instead of leaving it to the family and other institutions. Certain types of communication and traffic problems are commonly experienced. There is a need for a sophisticated system of education which must be undertaken by the state. The institutions never quite catch up with the problems which they are supposed to deal with. Riggs covers this point by describing it as a lack of 'congruence' between the institutions and their environment. In modern societies new problems constantly emerge which require adaptation by the institution and this adoption is often a slow business. To explain the time which it takes for the institutions to catch up is, of course, to explain the problem of structural modernisation.

The Barriers against Modernisation

The first proposition is that any structural change will be more difficult to accomplish than change which does not involve the alteration of the existing structure. By 'structural' change is meant alteration to the basic principles governing institutions. The more this change tends towards the replacement of the existing institutions with new ones the more difficult it will become. It would be comparatively easy for a welfare agency to change the level of benefits. It would be more difficult to reorganise the basis on which these benefits were given; let us say a change from the principle of 'less eligibility'. It would be more difficult still if the organisation had to reorganise its departments in order to deal with the new principles. This would certainly count as an institutional change but it would not be nearly as difficult as a change which involved the complete abolition of the existing institution and its replacement by a new type of welfare agency.

There have been vast changes in the powers and functions of local government since the end of the Second World War. Local authorities have lost services, such as hospitals outright, while other have been regionalised, such as water and police, and in virtually every service there has been a great injection of central control or guidance which has affected both standards and procedures. It was clear that a change of local government structure would solve many problems: planning or police are examples. Twenty-five years after the war only minor structural changes actually had taken place. Other devices, such as Ministry control, were used to overcome the problems to which an antiquated system made its contribution.

First, it is suggested that structural change is difficult because it involves very large alterations which people are cautious about. Secondly, structural change is closely linked to changes in the value system of the society. Thus changes in institutions will have or will appear to have implications for society begond the immedate events. Finally, those who owe their livelihood to the threatened institutions will be able to use these value implications to appeal against any new departures.

First, the importance for administrators of 'incremental change' has been described by Charles Lindblom and David Braybrook.[1] They point out that policy-makers commonly adopt the strategy of 'disjointed incrementalism' which of its nature deals with small changes rather than entertaining the possibility of large changes, the consequences of which are unknown.

They initially formulated their theory in answer to models of decision-making which had been suggested by workers in the fields of operational research or statistical decision theory. They point out that the conditions under which such models are appropriate are infrequent:

> . . . the hallmarks (of these conditions) are clarity of objective,
> explicitness of evaluation, a high degree of comprehensiveness of
> overview.[2]

They go on to argue that those conditions are not present when most
policy-makers are called on to take decisions. They have no clear idea
of the values which are involved and they have certainly not got e
extensive information about the consequences of their actions. In most
cases they take into account only a small fraction of the
alternative courses of action. Instead of the strategy which would
require wide knowledge or willingness to take large risks, decision-
makers use the strategy of incrementalism. They describe incrementalism
as the

> method of social action that takes existing reality as one
> alternative and compares the probable gains and losses or closely
> related alternatives by making relatively small adjustments in
> existing reality or making larger adjustments about whose
> consequences approximately as much is known as about the
> consequences of existing reality.[3]

Where the consequences of large increments are not known and the
present situation is undesirable, incrementalism gives way to
calculated risk. But this is a development which the decision-maker
tries to avoid. He does so by limiting himself to the consideration of
alternatives which marginally differ, from the situation, which, because
of some defect, he wants to change. The strategy is remedial rather
than one which tears down existing institutions in order to start
again. Lindblom also describes the strategy as 'exploratory' and 'serial'.[4]
A large change in policy is typically made by a series of small decisions
which makes small heuristic adjustments to the existing reality.

To conclude, Lindblom, Braybrook and Dahl give us one
explanation for the slowness in changing the structure of institutions.
Such a change is alien to the 'gradualist' way in which we are
accustomed to work and make decisions. In the terms just discussed
the decision to reorganise institutions is certainly a synoptic decision.
Decision-makers are accustomed to making adjustive changes in an
existing system. They operate within a system and are themselves part
of it. Since this is the case they will hesitate to uproot the system
irrespective of the problems it causes. Rather they will follow their
training to make further incremental changes to adjust and explore.
They are not trained to see things other than through the perspective
of the system and consequently will often be unable to see their
problems as coming from the basic structure of the system itself.

As far as the reform of local government is concerned, there can be
no question but that this is a major change and not just an incremental

one. It means there will be an upheaval in the administrative procedures for a very long time. Since the last major reorganisation took place in 1888 it was not very clear what might be the consequences of major reorganisation. It would be difficult to describe such an action as exploratory or serial. Once reform had taken place, it would be impossible to put the old councils back in power if the move turned out to be an error. These considerations therefore seem to point to the fact that local government reform was precisely the sort of development that one would not expect if Braybrook and Lindblom's account is a correct one.

The second difficulty in changing institutions is related. It may be seen by looking at the position of new countries.[5] Here is an example of a situation where a number of very large changes are made in political life as in various other aspects of the society. Barriers to modernisation in Asia and Africa often exist, not because those people lack the basic intelligence or even the technical skills, but because change in one institution may mean that their whole attitude to life is challenged. They may, for example, know perfectly well the principles of modern bureaucracy with its ideas of promotion on merit but at the same time be aware that they have extensive family commitments which must be honoured even if it means bending the system.[6]

One major reason why modernising *and* modern systems are so difficult to change is that they 'embody' the values of the system. In exactly this sense Milton Rockeach speaks about the 'belief-disbelief system for which institutions stand.'[7] Changing institutions is to challenge value in a way in which ordinary policy changes do not threaten them. This requires some explanation. If one studies any society there are many values which it seems to express in its life. These values are often expressed in vague and even contradictory senses. The British claim that they try to maintain individual freedom as well as social welfare, the rule of law as well as humanity in dealing with deviants. It may be protested that these are mere catch phrases. On the other hand, the interpretations which are made of these very general principles have been important for the way that legislation has been framed and is applied. The work of administrative theorists has taught us that values are not clearly held premises which uniquely determine the action to be taken. There are confusions about values and between the relative importance of different values.[8] It is much better to regard values as 'themes' which can be observed in human behaviour.

In a discussion of the administrative theory literature Murray Edelman gives the due to a link between values and institutions:

> Factual premises alone are certainly not sufficient to
> explain administrative decisional choices; but factual

premises in conjunction with observable role-taking are: for the
role both specifies the value premises operative in a
particular instance and establishes a probability that these same
value premises will be operative in future decision-making in the same
policy area.[9]

The roles, therefore, specify the values. Roles can only be seen in terms
of the institutions of the society, since institutions are the integration
of the roles of their members.[10]   Values are not prior to roles. They
emerge from role-taking, that is to say empirically observable
behaviour in an institutional setting. So far from the values being
given and the institutions established to express them or defend them,
values are in fact the rationalisation of our role-taking behaviour. Thus
values and the institutions (the organisation or role systems) are
closely linked.

In short, the decision-takers of every society observe value themes.
They are implicit in the roles that they perform. These values are
epitomised by such phrases as 'freedom of the individual', 'the
dictatorshop of the proletariat' and so on. The phrases, used so foten
on political platforms, are the verbal symbols used to refer to a
pattern of valued behaviour in the society.

It is not difficult to see why the reform of local government should
be so hard to accomplish. The closeness of the link between certain
values and the local institutions would mean that a proposals for
reform would raise all kinds of other considerations about the way
in which the society lived. A change of this magnitude may have been
necessary if modern services were to be run effectively. But an alteration
to the relationship between central and local government by new
regulations would not so openly challenge what were conceived as
central values. For evidence of this it is only necessary to read a few
columns in *Hansard* during debates when local government reforms
were being debated in the 1940s and 1950s. Virtually every speech is
filled with tributes to the worth of local government and the need
for local self-government for the British way of life. Members of
Parliament expressed points of view which were local and ministers
who answered the debates along with senior opposition spokesmen
also voiced these feelings whether they believed them or not. This
pattern of values may be real or simply perceived. That is to say, one
may distinguish between 'symbolic' vlaues and 'operational' values.
A 'symbolic' value is defined here as any value which is used as an
appeal for loyalty to the institution or which expressed the 'public
image' of the institution. A symbolic value 'identifies' the institution
in the public mind. It explains what the institution is *for* in theory.
An 'operational' value, on the other hand, is a value which is actually
performed by the institution. Thus, for example, local government may

be said to bear the symbolic value of local democracy and participation. The operational value of local government maybe that it carries out welfare and other services. A value expressed by an institution may be both symbolic and operational but there is a clear analytic difference. The importance of symbolic values in this study has to do with the fact that they are expressed not in one part of the life of the society, in the institutions to be modernised, but throughout the society. Thus when an attack is made on the existing institutions it can be made to appear that this value is being attacked in general. An institution which is being reformed because of deficiencies in one aspect of its operation may be defended by an appeal to a value which would not be endangered by the reform at all. The value appealed to will inevitably be that which has the most public appeal. Conversely, a case may be made for reform which appeals to a symbolic value when the aim of the reform is quite different. It is generally true, however, that it is easier to conserve institutions than to change them. The old symbolic values are ingrained. When there is a proposal to reorganise an institution the defenders of the *status quo* can more easily make it appear that the value symbolised by the institution is being attacked in general: that this attempt to reform is part of a conspiracy and so on. Among those less closely involved the reaction often is that it is impossible to know the side effects which the reform might have in terms of destroying the desired value. It is easier to leave things as they are. The institutions of a society express their symbolic values not only in verbal terms but in other more tangible and often more imposing ways. The courts are regarded as embodying the rule of law: the idea that each man is equal before the law. They are symbols for these values. More important for our purposes, they are very tangible symbols. They exist in time and space, they have buildings which are often awe-inspiring. They have officers who symbolise in their person the value discussed above. They are symbols of the most potent type. In the same way the councillors and the town hall and all the paraphernalia of local government are tangible symbols. It is easier to change the *functions* of the institutions than their form. Depending upon the importance of the value that is perceived to be at stake, a change in the form of the institution embodying that value will be difficult. To some extent these institutions reflect ourselves. In the case of local government we think of ourselves as coming from a particular part of a country. The institutions make it easier for us to conceptualise ourselves and the society in which we live. It was George Meade who drew attention to the importance of 'taking the role of the other'. It was this process of seeing one's own actions from the point of view of 'the significant other' which in fact created the image of the 'self'.

By . . . taking the attitude of the other toward his own gesture . . .

every gesture comes within a given social group of comments to
stand for a particular act or response, namely the act or response
which it calls forth explicitly in the individual to whom it is
addressed and implicitly in the individual who makes it: and this
particular act or response for which it stands is its meaning as a
significant symbol.[11]
We define our society in terms of the institutions which exist in it.
We define outselves to a large extent in terms of the society in which
we live: the roles we play: the functions we perform. Our self-image
as individuals is very much related to the institutions of society.
The more involved with these institutions one is, the more important
they are for the individual's self-image. Since politics is at least partially
about the wielding of power, political institutions like local government
will determine the self-image of people who are concerned with the
power relationships in a society.If one considers the people who
make up the institutions one comes upon the third difficulty in the way
of reform. By definition they are those most closely concerned with
and most skilled in public affairs. When policies or functions are
changed, there is little threat to their status. When the institution
itself is called in question and there are suggestions of structural
reforms there is a considerable threat. If the institution is to be
replaced with something different, their whole way of life is
qeustioned and their status (which may not be as high in the resulting
institution) and even their livelihood threatened. An attack on structure
will produce an extremely strong and skilful pressure group. It is
precisely these persons who, up to that time, have been regarded as the
guardians of a particular set of values in society.

David Schon approaches modernisation in a slightly different way.
In his Reith lectures[12] he points out[13] that every system has at least
three elements in it. There is a technology, a social structure made up
of roles and authority relationships and there is a theory. What Schon
describes as a theory has been discussed here as a value system. We may
say that the system, the institution, has a set of values which govern
the way in which different functionaries in the institution relate to
each other and to their environment. The point about the social
structure he illustrates by Sim's invention of continuous aim firing in
the US Navy. This disrupted the social structure of warships by
threatening the position of officers and skilled men operating the
ancient skills. Schon's discussion brings together the point about the
difficult of changing values (theory) with the point about threatening
the individual livelihoods of those involved.

The threat to the stability of established institutions carries
with it a threat to the stability of established theory and
ideology because institutions like the labour movement,

the church, social welfare agencies, all carry with them bodies of
theory, ways of looking at the world and when the institutions
are threatened, the bodies of theory are threatened as well.
Most important, when the anchors of institutions begin to be
loosened, the supports which it provides for the personal identity,
for the self, begin to be loosened too.[14]

Once more it is relatively easy to relate this point to what has already
been discussed about the reform of English local government. The
people challenged by the reform were important in the politics and
administration of English life. In the case of the full-time officers and
servants of the authority the argument is an economic one. If the plan
was for one local authority to take the place of three there could
only be one chief officer and at least two of the existing chiefs would
have to step down. This might not represent a financial loss but there
was a loss of status. For the men lower down the scale there were
other considerations. In their case it was arguable that there was a
dramatic curtailment of their prospects and therefore of their possible
earning power.

For the councillors there was no economic consideration, at least not
a direct one. They were concerned wholly with loss of status and an
interest in life. It is easy to condemn or ridicule people in this position.
Many councillors spend long hours in voluntary public work, but for
them politics may be their whole life.

Overcoming the Barriers

Under what sorts of circumstances will change come? Incremental
change cannot provide an answer to every problem. The strategy of
disjointed incrementalism is one which will only deal with a situation
in which it is widely accepted that the basic institutions are still
capable of doing their job. Many small decisions may be made which
may imperceptibly alter the functions or even the nature of an
institution. It may be that the institution successfully absorbs this
change and there is no need for a specific programme of reform. The
British Parliament has changed greatly since the days of the first
Hanoverians and yet these changes have usually taken place in a
piecemeal way. On very few occasions has there been a minor
alteration to the procedure or form of the House of Commons.[15]
Other institutions, however, have had to accept a traumatic change
or even replacement by something quite different. In Sweden, unlike
Britain, there was a very radical change in the nature of the legislature
when the old Estates were replaced by a modern bicameral system in
the nineteenth century.[16] Similarly in Britain the provisions and
institutions of the Elizabethan Poor Law were replaced when the

measures of 1834 came into effect. As far as the old Poor Law was concerned there simply were no further admustments which could make it acceptable in the changed conditions which the Industrial Revolution had brought.

As a general background to the institutional reform in the present day Schon points to the loss of 'the stable state'. He insists that innovation is today a commonplace and that the rate of diffusion of innovation is getting faster and faster. To this observation one would simply add that, even within this innovative century there are times when conditions appear to make change particularly acceptable.

The first step along the road to change is the development of a set of conditions which produces a group having an interest in change. The development of factories where large groups of workers had constant communication with each other led to the modern development of trade unions.[17] It is essential that the group should perceive the need for change and there is quite often a time lag between the appearance of the conditions and the recognition of a need for change. We may call such a group a 'demand group' in the sense that it is making a demand for a decision to be made in the field of public policy. Thus the first point is that a group develops having an interest in the performance of the institution in question but is not a part of it. This marginal status is crucial. They are involved with the function of the institution and they are interested in it. At the same time, being outside the institution, they can criticise it to a degree not to be entertained by members of the institution. Another point about the group is important. In so far as it owes its growth to a new feature of the society which is to be of growing importance, it too will increase in importance. Hence the values it embodies will also increase in importance.

The development of a separate profession of planning and the establishment of these planners at Whitehall as well as in local authority planning departments was the crucial ingredient of change in the reform being discussed here. In the early years after the war it was still true that planners had been trained in local authority departments usually as architects or engineers. It was only later that people were appointed with planning qualifications. Gradually more and more colleges and universities offered courses leading to a planning degree or certificate. Thus the old system of training on the job gave way to a pre-service training system. Inevitably this led to a less parochial outlook. The extent to which planners could move around to new jobs also contributed to this and, indeed, this was a consideration which applied to many senior local government officers. Officers were no longer as likely to retire from the same authority as that which recruited them. In the case of planners the mobility was, perhaps, that much greater since they were so much in demand. In many if not all schools, students were taught to consider planning in a regional context. The existence of a local government boundary was often disregarded. The idea of regional planning was important and was to become more so as the years went on. Regional economic planning boosted the interest and the importance of the region for physical planners.

Thus there existed a group of professionals in the counties and county boroughs who were trained to see beyond their own boundaries. Many of them inevitably became critical of the constraints which these boundaries placed upon the practice of their profession.

A development of at least as great an importance was the interest taken by the central government in planning. From the early days of the Ministry of Town and Country Planning there was an involvement in this field. Part of it was an encouragement to local authorities to come together in Joint Boards or Committees for regional or at least co-operative planning. In the 'sixties we have seen that more direct action was taken. Ministry exercises were mounted to look at the South East and at other parts of the country and Planning Teams, drawn partly from local authority staff but also from the Ministry, worked in many parts of the country. This development meant the creation of a group of experts with an interest in the operation of the unit to be reformed but without, in the case of the civil servants, a commitment to a particular type of organisation and, therefore, an openess to and perhaps even an enthusiasm for reform.

The next step on the way to change depends upon the extent to which this group has some influence upon decision-making in the society. To have much hope of success, demands for major changes in policy must be made by groups having access to the decision-making processes. Historically they may have been initiated by groups or individuals outside these processes but until they are adopted by a group having this access they are not likely to be successful. It may happen that, as with the trade unions in Britain, a group making a demand from outside eventually becomes a member of the elite itself and thus is in a much stronger position.

The degree of influence which any group has will vary from issue to issue. It will also depend upon the other groups who are opposed to it or who have some peculiar point of view of their own. Nevertheless, there are certain resources which a group may have which will be important for its power *vis-à-vis* the rest. It has already been suggested that the acceptability of the group to other groups having access to decision-making is important. Anybody coming from outside the world of politics to press for a policy not only has to learn the

rules of the game but also has to be accepted as a serious contender
by those who themselves are concerned with politics. In short, the
position of any group in the eyes of members of other groups is of the
foremost importance.[18] It may be that the others have an incorrect
appreciation of the power of this particular group. If they exaggerate
its power then they may concede more than they need. Apart from
the perceived power of any particular group there is the traditional
respect in which it is held. This respect may well mean that its
competitors do not press their full advantage.

These points are particularly important to a discussion of structural
reform. It has already been pointed out that this type of reform
threatens a particularly important group, namely those who are
responsible for the running of the institution, which is an important
part of the society, they will have the respect due to the
legitimising character of the institution. Any attempt to reform the
institution will therefore come against strong opposition. This means
that successful opposition to them will have to come from groups of
at least equal power and status.

The influence of the local government officers and councillors was
great. They had political influence and they were recognised as
important figures in the administration of government services. The
local government associations were always consulted and their views
were of considerable significance. If such a situation had persisted it is
unlikely that reform of local government would have taken place.
With the arrival of a Labour Government committed to reform of many
aspects of British life there came the impetus for this sort of change.
Only the government of the day had sufficient political status to
legitimise reform on this scale. Once they had decided to do something
not even the reputedly powerful local government associations could
do anything to stop it.

The legitimacy of those defending the institution from reform
depends upon the way in which the institution is seen to embody values
which are important to society. The most dangerous challenge to
an institution is posed at a time when new values come into vogue
which it does not represent and to which it may even be hostile.
Equality of all before the law was denied by the Estates system
prevalent with the end of the nineteenth-century in many parts of
Europe. This arrangement was replaced by a legislature in which all
were more or less equal. Reform of an institution will be accelerated
when the new values it does not represent become so important that
they are supported by more than one group. In other words the
'cultural profile' of society changes to such an extent that groups in the
elite have an interest in pressing for this new value. Among many
members of the elite and especially among governmental elite there

will be great reluctance to make the change since the defenders of the institution to be reformed have been colleagues in the past and reform will mean partial dislocation of the system which all have learned to work. This consideration will decline in importance with the increasing perception of need for the new value. The final blow will come when members of the governmental elite press for reform because it has adopted the new value. The attack on a governmental institution by one or several other governmental institutions marks the final stage on the way to reform.

Until the mid-'sixties the conditions did not exist under which a British government would have wanted to go through the trouble caused by reform.

But the symbols used by the Labour Party in their election campaign and in their subsequent speeches embodied the value of modernisation, efficiency, and technological change, values which local government was not perceived to share. Secondly, Labour's local election losses in 1967 and 1968 meant that there were fewer Labour representatives in local government whose status would be challenged by reform. So government was given the will and the means to reform.

Conclusion

The institutions of local government express certain values in British society of which the safeguarding of local democracy is the most important. The British would agree that central administration from London with no local government would be undemocratic.[19] Some would go much further and say that local government was the main bastion of our liberties against an encroaching bureaucracy. So when central government attempts to alter local government it meets great difficulties. As a spokesman for an interest, local authorities have a legitimacy which other spokesmen simply do not have. It is also obvious that local councillors and officers constitute an important group defending the *status quo*.

How were these strong figures finally challenged? The development of new values in the provision of social welfare and economic planning suggested that the units of local government were too small. In 1888 local authorities ran few and limited services as compared to the present day. An additional problem was the increased demand for specialist services and officers who could administer them. The largest authorities could attract the best administrators and, at least in the eyes of Whitehall, did the best job.

It was, however, the development of planning and the wide application of this notion in many spheres of British life which was that final and most important consideration. Small authorities could make joint arrangement for the provision of many of the other services but it was impossible to plan an area physically or economically on this *ad hoc* basis. Joint standing committees for regional plans had for long been virtually inoperative. There could be no solution short of overall reorganisation. The shortage of land and other resources was becoming more evident. The fact that the civil servants who were bureaucratically cautious of change now recognised the need for planning made it almost inevitable that change would come.

So the English local government system was changed even though not as radically as once was planned. The demands of a new type of society, supported by powerful interests and expressed in terms of new symbols, were able to make a fundamental change to the pattern of government in Britain.

NOTES

1.   David Braybrook and Charles Lindblom. *A Strategy for Decision: Policy Evaluation as a Social Process,* Glencoe Free Press, Glencoe, 1963. See also Robert A. Dahl and Charles Lindblom, *Politics, Economics and Welfare,* Harper Torchbooks, New York, 1953.
2.   Braybrook and Lindblom, p.340.
3.   Dahl and Lindblom, p. 82.
4.   Braybrook and Lindblom, p. 71.
5.   Lucien Pye, *Political Culture and Political Development,* Princeton University Press, Princeton, New Jersey, 1965. James Coleman, *Nigeria,* University of California Press, Berkeley, 1958.
6.   Gerald E. Caiden, *Administrative Reform,* Aldine, Chicago, 1969.
7.   Milton Rokeach, *The Open and Closed Mind,* Michigan State University Press; E. Lansing, Michigan, 1960, p. 68.
8.   See, for example, the work of Herbert Simon, *Administrative Behaviour,* Macmillan, New York, 1957.
9.   Murray Edelman, *The Symbolic Uses of Politics,* University of Illinois Press, Urbana, 1964.
10.   In this discussion Edelman is heavily dependent on G.H. Meade. See, for example, *Mind, Self and Society,* University of Chicago Press, Chicago, 1934.
11.   Ibid., p. 47.
12.   BBC, 1970-71. Published in *The Listener,* 1970.
13.   Ibid., p.724.
14.   Ibid., p. 687
15.   See Sir I. Jennings, *Parliament,* Cambridge University Press, London, 1957.
16.   There is an account of this in D. Rostow, *The Politics of Compromise,* Princeton University Press, Princeton, New Jersey, 1955, Chapter 1.

17. This point is well brought out in Martin Harrison, *Trade Unions and the Labour Party,* Allen and Unwin, London, 1960.

18. See David Truman, *The Governmental Process*, Knopf, New York, 1958.

19. For discussions of the theory of local government see William J.M. Mackenzie, *Theories of Local Government,* London School of Economics, London, Greater London Paper no. 2, 1961, and L. James Sharpe, 'Theories and Values of Local Government', *Political Studies,* vol. XVIII, no. 2, June 1970.

APPENDIX 1   DRAMATIS PERSONAE

Ministers with Responsibility for Local Government

1944	Minister of Health	Henry Willink
	Lord Privy Seal	Sir W. A. Jowitt
		(chaired a Committee of Enquiry into the reorganisation of local government)
1945	Minister of Health	Aneurin Bevan
	Parliamentary Secretary	Charles W. Kay
1948	Minister of Health	Arthur Blenkinsop
1950	Minister of Health	Hilary Marquand
1951	Minister of Housing and Local Government	Harold Macmillan
1954	Minister of Housing and Local Government	Duncan Sandys
1957	Minister of Housing and Local Goverment	Henry Brooke
1961	Minister of Housing and Local Government	Charles Hill
1962	Minister of Housing and Local Government	Sir Keith Joseph
1964	Minister of Housing and Local Government	Richard Crossman
1966	Minister of Housing and Local Government	Anthony Greenwood
1969	Minister of Local Government and Regional Planning	Anthony Crosland
1970	Secretary of State for the Environment	Peter Walker
	Minister of Local Government and Development	Graham Page
1972	Secretary of State for the Environment	Geoffrey Rippon
1973	Minister of Housing and Local Government	Graham Page
1974	Secretary of State for the Environment	Anthony Crosland

Secretaries of the Local Government Associations

1939-45 County Councils Association	Sir Sidney Johnson

1945-64 County Councils Association	W.L. Dacey
1964-74	A.C. Hetherington
1939-45 Association of Municipal Corporations	Sir Harry Pritchard
1945-62	Sir Harold Banwell
1962-73	J.C. Swaffield
1973-74	R.H. McCall
1949-70 Urban District Council Association (formed in 1949)	H.S. Haslam
1970-72	F. Barnes
1972-74	W.R. Warrington
1949-59 Rural District Councils Association	John J. MacIntyre
1959-74	S. Rhodes

On 1 April 1974 the following new local government associations were formed as successors to the previous bodies

Association of County Councils	A.C. Hetherington
Association of Metropolitan Authorities	R.H. McCall
Association of District Councils	S Rhodes.

APPENDIX 2   THE DISTRIBUTION OF FUNCTIONS: NEW AND OLD VERSIONS

It may be useful to outline the way in which the different functions were distributed among the authorities under the local government system which existed up to 1974, under the Maud Commission proposals (published in 1969) and the new form of government which was established in 1974.

In the system up to 1974 the county councils carried the main functions as will be seen in the table overleaf, while the less important local government functions were carried out by authorities of various sorts: municipal boroughs, urban districts and rural districts. There were also parishes in rural areas which had a limited range of functions. The county boroughs (on the whole the largest towns) had a full range of local government functions.

The Maud Commission recommended that local government should be carried on by unitary authorities but it also recommended the establishment of three special metropolitan areas in which local government would be split between the metropolitan council and the metropolitan district councils: Birmingham with seven districts, Liverpool with four districts and Manchester with nine districts. In addition there were to be eight provinces elected by the councils of the metropolitan areas and the unitary areas with power to co-opt members. These would have responsibilities for economic planning and would have settled the provincial planning strategy as well as the development of further education and special education.

Community councils were also recommended to be sounding boards for the electorate.

The 1974 reform introduced a system in which there were counties and county districts. Their powers are laid out in the table overleaf. There were also to be six metropolitan areas with metropolitan district councils. But the distribution of functions between these two was different from the distribution which was envisaged by Maud.

Main Outline of Structure

Local Government System in 1973

Large towns: County Borough Councils

Rest: County Councils
     County District Councils
     (Municipal Boroughs)
     (Urban Districts)
     (Rural Districts)
     Parish Councils in rural areas

Division of Functions

County Borough Councils: all local
government powers.

Redcliffe Maud Recommendations

Metropolitan Areas: 3 Metropolitan Area
Councils, Metropolitan District Councils

Rest: 58 Unitary Area Councils
     Local Councils in all areas
     Provincial Councils

Unitary Area Councils: all local
government powers

Metropolitan Councils
(a) Planning
    Building regulations
    Transportation
    Intelligence
(b) Metropolitan housing policy
    Tenant selection policy
    Rent policy
    Residual housing power
(c) Water supply
    Main sewage
    Sewage disposal
    Refuse disposal
    Clean Air Acts
(d) Arts, entertainment, sports and
    recreation policy
(e) Police
    Fire
    Ambulance
(f) Co-ordinated investment
    in metropolitan areas

Metropolitan District Councils:
(a) Education
    Libraries
    Youth employment
(b) Personal social service
    Personal health service
    House building
    Housing management
(c) Local sewers and drains
    Refuse collection
    Cemeteries and crematoriums
    Coast protection

1973 Local Government Act

Metropolitan Areas: Metropolitan Area
Councils, Metropolitan District Councils

Rest: County Councils
     County District Councils
     Community Councils in rural areas
     and small free-standing towns with
     a possible extension elsewhere

Metropolitan Councils
(a) Strategic planning
    Building regulations
    Highways
    Transportation
    Intelligence
(b) Housing reserve power
(c) Arts, entertainment, sports,
    parks and recreation
(d) Police
    Fire
    Ambulance
(e) Weights and measures
    Food and drugs
    Clean air
    Refuse disposal
    Environmental health

Metropolitan District Councils:
(a) Education
    Libraries
    Youth employment
(b) Environmental health
    Refuse collection
(c) Local planning
(d) Sewers
(e) Arts, entertainment and sports
(f) Personal social service

(d) Arts, entertainment, sports etc.
(e) Food and drugs
Weights and measures
Consumer protection
Shops Acts
Licences
Registration

County Councils:
Planning
Development control
Highways
Transport
Police
Education
Libraries
Personal social services
Fire
Weights and measures
Food and drugs
Smoke abatement
Refuse disposal
Environment health
Arts, sports, cultural Parks and open open spaces
Playing fields and swimming baths

District Councils:
Coast protection
Housing
Local streets
Refuse collection
Environmental health
Parks and open spaces
Museum and art galleries
Playing fields and swimming baths

County Councils:
Planning
Education
Libraries
Child care
Police
Fire
Ambulance
Probation
Weights and measures
Food and drugs
Public health
Personal social services
Licencing
Parks and recreation, arts
Youth employment

County District Councils:
(functions varied with type)
M = Municipal Borough
U = Urban District
Food and drugs
Coast protection
Housing
Building regulations
Nuisances
Sewerage
Street lighting (permissions)
Refuse collection
Refuse disposal
Cemeteries and crematoriums
Parks, entertainment, cultural sports
Libraries, M.U.
Local roads, M.U.
Swimming baths
Smoke abatement
Rating (may have additional delegated services)

Maud compared with the Conservative Government's Proposals

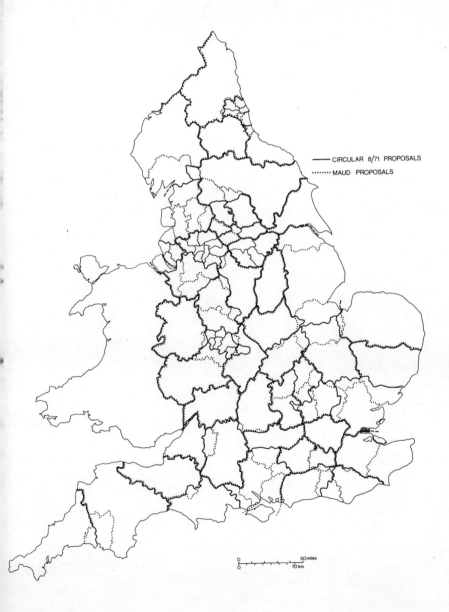

CIRCULAR 8/71 PROPOSALS

MAUD PROPOSALS

50miles

70 km

INDEX

Abercrombie, Sir Patrick, 21
Agriculture, 23, 31
Aldermen, 82
Altrincham, 77
*Area and Status of Local
    Authorities in England and
    Wales,* 48
Arnold-Baker, Charles, 71
Ashworth, H., 15
Association of Municipal
    Corporations (AMC), 40; and the
    1957 White Papers 116-17; and
    the Local Government Boundary
    Commission 102-8; and the
    Local Government Commission,
    119-23; and the Redcliffe Maud
    Commission 123-8; calls for a
    Royal Commission 99, 106, 112;
    divisions within 89-90, 102,
    104-6; failure to agree on policy,
    91, 96, 115; favours a one-tier
    system, 96-7, 99, 110, 112;
    favours city regions, 54;
    foundation, 88-9; national
    political parties' role in, 135;
    officers, 90; proposals submitted
    in *1942,* 96-7, 99; smaller
    members, 119; reaction to the
    1970 and *1971* White Papers, 128.

Banwell, Sir Harold, 90, 109, 111,
    117.
Barlow report, *Distribution of the
    Industrial Population,* 18, 20-21,
    24
Basingstoke, 76
Berkshire, 75-6
Bevan, Aneurin, 42, 45-6, 104, 106,
    139-40
Birmingham, 70, 77, 90, 165
Blenkinsop, Arthur, 46
Block grants, 49-50
Board of Trade, 21, 27-30 *passim*
Bolton, 77
Bolton, J.E., 64
Boundaries, 26; alteration of, after
    the Redcliffe Maud Commission

report, 79-80; commissions, 41-54;
conflict between the counties and
county boroughs, 12-13, 103-8,
119-20; factors affecting
extensions, 51, 108. *see also*
Local Government Boundary
Commission *and* Local
Government Commission
Bradford, 76
Braybook, David, 150-51
Briggs, Asa, 19
Brighton, 80
Brown, George, 122
Buchanan Report, *Traffic in Towns,*
    34, 57-9
Burns, John, 15
Bury, 77

Central government: as the initiator
    of reform, 102, 129; becomes
    committed to planning, 30;
    control of industrial location, 30;
    control over local authorities,
    9, 46; financial controls, 48-9;
    interest in planning, 158;
    ministers responsible for local
    government, 163; ministries and
    reform, 38-87; reluctance to
    initiate reform, 114; *see also
    specific ministries*
Cheshire, 126, 141
Chetwynd, George, 32
Cities: fear of, 18-19; population
    loss from, 19, 20; *see also*
    conurbations *and* urban areas
City regions, 53-4, 65; and the
    Redcliffe Maud commission
    69-70, 73.
Coast protection, 79
Cole, 41
Community Councils, 73, 81
Committee system, 62; after
    reform, 83
Community councils, 146, 165
Compton, Sir Edmund, 82
Conservative government *1970-74,*
    78-84; implementation of

171